GOLD

AUTO-BIOGRAPHY OF A SUFI

IDHHB, INC. PUBLISHERS

THE SLEEPING SUFI LYING IN STATE AT THE CRESTLINE ASHRAM
FEBRUARY 1972

CONTENTS

FOREWORD
by Mr. A. Harkounian

"Now I realize full satisfaction with my life here on the Earth, having completed my labors for the benefit of all beings by introducing into the life of man the data which can make possible the attainment of conscious life . . . "

G. wrote those words as he began the third book of Creation Story Verbatim on October 30, 1949, following an extraordinary series of events in which he entered into periodic states of trance and seemed to be in communication with someone unseen.

Everyone was surprised, then, when he suddenly ceased writing, leaving that book and the other two books in the series, A Procession of Fools, and The Ninety-Nine Names of Nothing (both to be released soon) in first draft form.

Finally now in January of 1972 he has again taken up writing on these books and has completed them in publishable form. Creation Story was released publicly in partial form, but will not be available in its full and final version except to Study Groups.

And so it remains for those not in Study Groups to delve into this present volume to discover for oneself the deep causes of the arising of conscious purpose and will in Mr. Gold's life as he saw it arise and unfold within himself.

He describes quite a few intimate personal details of his inner life as he tells us about the outer and inner experiences which led him on his search, and through his powerful imagery he conjures up for us our own obligation to search for truth no matter where the path may lead us.

The ideas presented in this volume do not belong to any one group, nor to any single teacher, but to everyone everywhere in the New Age. They call us to transformation of ourselves, to the active participation in the pageant of conscious life.

Because life today has become so mechanized, those efforts which one would ordinarily make toward conscious life have been eliminated, and so special conditions must be introduced artificially through schools.

This book represents such a school, but does not and cannot outline it in workbook form. In this volume the reader will see the result—although hidden in some ways—of more than twenty-five years of work.

The original trilogy was divided into three major categories of work:

The first book, Avatar's Handbook, was intended to constrain the mind to release certain cultural beliefs, attitudes and habits, and to introduce a few school ideas.

The second book, Tales of Mother Beast, was intended to provide the inner shocks necessary for the arousal of a new kind of inner energy.

The third book, Creation Story Verbatim, was intended to provide the material for The New Life—introduction of the method of fusing the three ordinary centers, thinking, feeling and motor functions, into a unified and whole being.

Some material from these first two books have been included here, and the remainder placed within the revised and expanded New, Improved Creation Story Verbatim, for the use of Study Groups.

INTRODUCTION
by Cybele Gold

The summer of '67 on a warm mid-June afternoon. I was walking down a side street off Hollywood Boulevard when I passed by a place called the Psychedelic Supermarket.

I heard the sounds of rock music streaming out of the open door, and looked inside. I saw lots of people browsing around at different booths, each of which showed their specialty. The atmosphere was dark and moody, and the cool air-conditioned breeze felt inviting after the outdoor heat of Los Angeles.

When I walked inside I could see the things that were on display—far out posters, light shows for the home, beaded jewelry, creatively shaped candles, printed T-shirts, Indian clothing, and of course the old standard . . . roach clips.

As I entered I saw something familiar over my right shoulder—an old showcase displaying essential oils, candles, incense, old manuscripts and other impressive items. So these had been the source of that incredibly fragrant smell that had reached me when I stood on the sidewalk outside, I thought.

It looked to me like an occult shop. I'm from New Orleans, where occult shops are disguised as religious stores or pharmacies. Of course this caught my attention and curiosity, for I loved to dabble in the arts.

The space was small—about ten feet by ten feet. On my left were shelves filled with occult and metaphysical books lighted by small pin spotlights. On my right was a curtained off area. I had no idea what was behind that curtain.

Just then, Mr. Gold came out, cradling a box filled with vials of different essential oils which he proceeded to put in the showcase. The perfumed odor permeated the area with its intoxicating effects. They were the best oils and perfume I had ever found.

When he finished what he was doing he looked up at me, and said, "Well, are you ready to get to work this lifetime?"

What could I say? I was completely shocked and experienced a great sigh of relief, feeling that I might have actually found someone who could ask me the question that I was beginning to think I would never hear. Do you think that I would hesitate on that offer? Not on my life. "Boy, am I ever ready!" I replied.

I felt that lonely and puzzled condition in which I had been living since I was five years old suddenly vanish. Now I could begin. I knew that he had offered the help and guidance I needed and that he actually had the ability to bring about the conditions necessary for spiritual development.

He said that it would be three years to the day before I could start to work.

"What?" I exploded. "But I'm ready now!"

"First you must develop the background and language to understand my methods," he replied. "And even though you may be ready to learn, I am not ready to teach."

He also explained that I needed to acquire a strong self-discipline over my personal comforts and desires. I knew that what he was saying was true from my own observation of myself. He then asked me if I wanted to live or to die.

I replied that I wanted to live. I had that sinking feeling in the pit of my stomach when I realized that by saying this I had agreed to begin. All of a sudden I saw before me the enormous effort that I would have to make just to get ready to work.

"It seems impossible only because you are now standing still," he said suddenly. "Once you move from there you will find it easy to make efforts."

"How did you know that was what I was thinking about?" I asked, annoyed and a little upset. I began trying to hold down all the thoughts I didn't want anyone else to know about, realizing at the same time that this probably made it more obvious.

"I always know what you are thinking," he said, "because I always know what I am thinking."

For a moment I saw the road before me, and realized that there was no end to it, once begun. There was no question now that I had begun working toward the horizon, knowing that it can never be reached, but that the struggle itself transforms one into a higher being. To really live a life . . . my life . . . that would be quite an accomplishment. This meeting was the start of an incredible relationship.

Nothing else was said at that point; he just went back to work getting his shop ready for customers.

I left the shop and started toward my car, thinking as I walked of what had just happened and remembering how familiar he had felt to me. He looked like a mad scientist. His hair was all frizzed out as if he had stuck his finger in an electric socket. It was tightly curled and stuck out all over, except for the very crown of his head, upon which no hair of any kind was present. His eyes were just open pools of tranquility. The certainty and childish playful innocence that is not commonly seen in the eyes of most people that inhabit this planet Earth was a joyful surprise for me.

His body was plump but strong. His clothing was a mess. His shirt was long-sleeved and gray in color—and that was not the original color, either. It was torn in spots. His tan Levis were worn and also very dirty. He was greasy looking and smelled of sweat.

Since I was not used to associating with people who resembled human grizzly bears, I thought that it would be okay to study with him . . . as long as I could do it at a distance.

I started going to the shop about four times a week. During most of this time he would be engaged in conversation with someone, and these would go on and on for hours.

I would sit or walk around, waiting for him to have some spare time to talk with me. When I became impatient and approached him with questions about spiritual ideas, he would change the subject to what seemed to me to be ordinary ideas, or jokes and stories which had no real bearing on the subject.

Another thing is that in order to approach him in any other way, one had to buy something in his shop. I had no real idea of the type of communication he was using, for I was a very serious person and he seemed to always be joking and taking everything around him as absurdities. This was upsetting to me, because I felt that my life, my time, and what was to become of me were very important. How frustrated I used to get with him.

As time went on and on and on . . . I got the reading list and began to acquire the necessary background. After two years I was invited to attend a class that was held only on Thursday nights at seven-thirty sharp at the Markham building on Cosmo Street in Hollywood. "Couldn't be a better choice of location," I thought.

When I walked in there were a few people standing in the lobby waiting for the elevator. They didn't say anything to me; they just talked quiety among themselves. I looked around to see if there was anything posted that would help me find out where the class was taking place, but there were no signs or notices. I decided that these people must be going to the same place, so I waited to see where they were going.

The floor was marble. There was a winding staircase going to heaven knows where. All one could see was the first ten steps, and above that was total darkness. The air was damp and cool in the building. I was looking up, staring at the chandelier, when I heard a "kerthunk". The elevator had arrived. . . and what an elevator! It shook and rattled as we got inside, and then the door had to be opened by hand, the second door held, and then both doors forced closed while you pushed the button for the floor you wished.

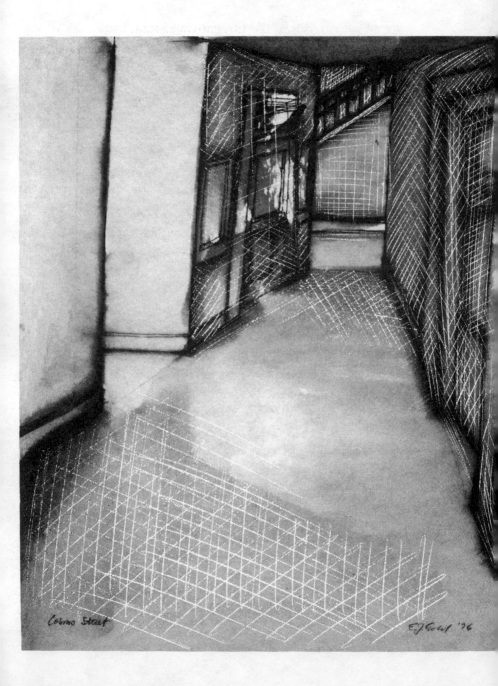

We all squeezed into the tiny moving room, the doors were closed, and someone pressed the third floor button. We rose slowly and precariously. It seemed as though it took us at least five minutes to reach the third floor.

Everyone got out and went straight across the hall to a very dark room, lit only by an amber-colored lamp and one candle that burned on a small table to the left of Mr. Gold.

He was seated on the floor, still in the same type of clothing and smelling as usual. Incense poured out of a bowl that was next to the candle. He sat with his legs crossed Indian fashion, smoking a cigarette.

The other people went in and seated themselves quietly and waited for Mr. Gold to begin. I noticed the old tattered Persian carpet hanging on the wall behind him. The mystery was intense and the odor was musky and pungent.

At ten P.M. Mr. Gold suddenly got up and left the room and disappeared for the night. I thought he might be up to his old tricks or that it was a lesson that I had missed. The people that were in the room with me began to docilely file out into that weird elevator again to return to the streets of Hollywood. I stayed around for a little while longer, trying to recap what I could remember about this meeting.

After I was tired of thinking and still couldn't come to any real conclusion about what had happened, I decided to go home. I got into the elevator that was destined to become a constant companion in my life and pressed the main-floor button.

Downstairs, as I opened the door to leave, I saw Mr. Gold talking to a friend of his. I walked up to him and said good night and introduced myself to the other man. "His name is Saint Mike," Mr. Gold said.

32) THIRD FLOOR HALLWAY, 1976   8"x10"

Cosmo Street

They invited me for some coffee and food at a restaurant on Hollywood Boulevard not far from Cosmo Street. This was an incredible space. It was filled with many people of the street. Ladies of the evening, men of the evening, pimps, costumed sword-and-sorcery fans, and us. "Oh, terrific! What a night this has been," I said to myself. I looked up and saw Mr. Gold's expression of amusement at the situation. I relaxed a bit and tried to decide what to order. The outcome was a glass of cola.

Mr. Gold and Saint Mike ordered hamburgers and fries and coffee. I was quietly watching them observing the goings-on of the restaurant. It was unbelievable! People were actually selling dope and people to one another over the counter.

When the waitress brought the food to the table it was the greasiest hamburger that I've ever seen. The men ate their food without any complaints and I sat sipping my drink. I remember thinking, "Why would they want to eat in a place like this? For what reason?" I asked him these questions and he replied that I need not know this yet, just notice the interactions that were taking place in the restaurant.

I agreed to this and sat attentively, trying to see beyond the obvious. There was a game we played in class called "What's wrong with this picture?". I began to use this concept to see what could be seen here. I sat there for about ten minutes more and suddenly Mr. Gold and Saint Mike said that it was time for them to go and that they would walk me to my car.

I gathered my things and walked with them to the cashier and then out the door and down the street toward my car. When we arrived at my car, they said goodnight, and Mr. Gold said that I could come to the ten o'clock Saturday morning class at Cosmo if I wished. Then they turned and walked out of my sight. I started up the car engine and drove home thinking, "Well, I will understand what he did and why someday."

34) COSMO STREET FROM ABOVE, 1976 9"x12"

Saturday I went to class. Saint Mike was there along with ten other people I hadn't seen there before. For the next three hours Saint Mike asked the question "Why are you here?" over and over again. I got angry and thought he must be crazy, because we had already answered him many times.

Then suddenly I realized why he was asking that question over and over. It was so that people could take a really good look at why they thought they wished to be there with Mr. Gold and to decide if that was what they really wished for themselves.

"You know why he asks this question again?" asked Mr. Gold. "Because you aren't telling the truth."

"But we *are* telling the truth," someone objected.

"No you're not," said Saint Mike. "You're only telling the truth as you know it. You don't know how to tell the truth."

After that, I didn't feel angry any more, but I still thought they were both a little crazy.

"Why did you come here?" continued Saint Mike. "Look around. It's just an empty room. What do you think you can get here? What do you think is being offered?"

"Where do you think you are right now?" asked Mr.

Gold.

"In an office on Cosmo Street," said one.

"In the Markham Building, above Hollywood Boulevard," said another.

"See?" said Saint Mike. "You don't know how to tell the truth."

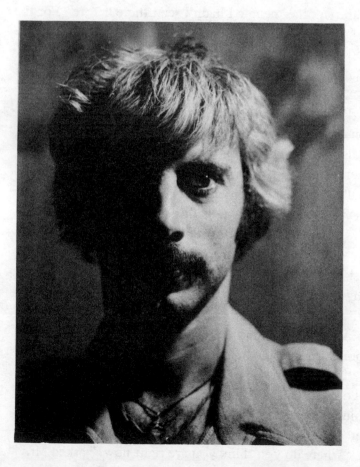

I went to Cosmo for two and a half years, most of which
was spent finding out why I was there, until I was invited
to move up to Crestline with a work group.

Crestline is a small community in the San Bernardino
mountains where you can hear the birds sing, see squirrels
running up and down the trees, bears rummaging around
the property at night, raccoons that will come up to you
and take food right from your hand, and beautiful blue
skies and clear air. That sure was an improvement over
all that L.A. smog and traffic noise.

The day I was invited to come up to Crestline I couldn't
make it, but I said that I would be along as soon as I could
finish up my karmic debts in the city.

I often wondered what went on that day in Crestline.
It was policy that the group never discuss with another
any class that was not attended by him or her. We were
not even allowed to take tape recorders or notebooks into
a class or discuss among ourselves what we thought Mr.
Gold meant by what he had said. These classes were for
those attending and no one else. We weren't trying to be
secretive; it just didn't apply to any other individual, and
if it did it would be given to them in their own time.

Mr. Gold and a group of people had moved up to the mountains, although Cosmo was still being run by a couple who were his students. He would occasionally show up. One would never know when he might walk through that door.

I went to Cosmo Street that night for the last time. I went in as usual and sat down. As I sat there, I began to feel a little strange about being there. The environment of the room began to change from that old musky room to the smell and feeling of the fresh night air of the mountains. I saw Mr. Gold and a group of my fellow students in class at the house called Maison Rouge in Crestline. I could hear Mr. Gold talking. I was no longer sitting in Cosmo Street, but in Crestline.

I told the couple that was heading the class in Cosmo that I had to get up to Crestline right away before it was too late. I had a definite feeling that if I waited and didn't go now it would be much harder or impossible later on.

So I went to my car, drove home, packed a weekend bag, got my dog and left my apartment. I got on the super slab toward San Bernardino. It was about midnight then, and I knew that the students in Crestline were on a schedule starting at 3:00 A.M. and retiring at 11:00 P.M., so I thought that everyone would be asleep when I would frantically land there with my suitcase and my dog in the middle of the night.

Although I knew that the schedule would mean that everyone would have retired hours ago, I kept seeing Mr. Gold standing down at the Study House with his arms wide open, greeting me.

I drove up, turned off the ignition, and waited for my eyes to adjust to the evening darkness. I got out of my car a nervous wreck and started to walk to the Maison Rouge, when I saw Mr. Gold standing on the last step next to the Study House, with his arms open wide just as I had pictured him.

I ran into his arms with tears flooding down my cheeks, saying, "Please help me, I am dying and I want to live."

He said that I was not to worry, that I had come just in time, and that it would happen this time as long as I continued my work.

We went inside the Study House and I entered into the meditation exercise that the other students were doing at that time. That was June 13th, 1970, exactly three years to the day from the moment we met.

The following day, the Cosmo Street meeting house was closed, with no forwarding address.

After the meditation in the Study House was complete
for the night the rest of the students and I walked up the
stone steps toward the main house. It was around two-thirty
in the early morning. The night sky was lit by the brilliance
of the full moon, and millions of tiny pinholes of bluish-
white light radiated above the trees and reflected on the still,
natural wooded environment. It was so beautiful and peace-
ful I stood at the top of the stairs for a few minutes to look,
listen, smell, feel and sense it all.

As I got to the front door of the Maison Rouge, I felt as
if I had returned home to my family after a very long journey. I opened the door and went into the main room. At
that time the downstairs consisted of one large room measuring fifteen by twenty-five feet, and a very small kitchen
fifteen by six feet. Upstairs there was a small bathroom
which was equipped with a toilet, sink, shower, and a bare
lightbulb hanging above a mirror. Three tiny bedrooms, each
measuring only six by eight feet, completed the upper floor.

One of the bedrooms, the first one at the head of the
stairs, was Mr. Gold's. The next two bedrooms were staff
dorms. There were two double bunks in each room, and
just enough room to squeeze by to get in and out. The main
room downstairs was not just a meeting and dining room.

Along the walls were four double bunk beds, a double bed, and a picnic table with two long benches. Every bed was taken except for the double bed downstairs. "Well," I guessed, "this is to be my bed . . . for a while anyway."

The students wasted no time in getting themselves ready for bed. There was no excessive talking or dawdling ever at Maision Rouge. No one would ever think of indulging in unnecessary chatter. There were no radios or television sets present—only a library filled with science fiction and metaphysical books.

When you weren't working, cleaning, doing seated meditations, moving exercises, group readings, and group study periods, you were reading to gather data and background in order to understand what one usually experienced while working with Mr. Gold.

Working with him—if he accepted you as a student—was the hardest and most grueling task that you could take on in this lifetime. At least that was how most of the students felt about it. He is a determined and ruthless fanatic about the work, and if one can't handle his manifestations on this level then one has to leave. He always told us that the door was open from the inside, and that we could leave any time we decided it was no longer profitable or possible to stay.

Living at Maison Rouge under these conditions was definitely something I was going to have to work out with myself. There was no place to run to if I got uncomfortable. I would just have to stay and confront the situation.

I knew that there were going to be times when I would be uncomfortable, and maybe even worse. I made the decision not to live a life of self-indulgence, but one of service.

I got into bed and lay there looking around the space that was going to be my home. There was a bare bulb burning under the balcony that was the only source of light for the downstairs room except for the fireplace on cold nights.

It got cold pretty often because the house was over a mile above sea level, and it was almost always foggy in the morning. It reminded me of being in Japan.

Mr. Gold asked me if I would like to come up to his room and talk for a while, if I was feeling like having some company. I had never seen or met most of the students that were there. I thanked him for his offer and said that I was doing fine and that I was tired enough to collapse for the night.

"Okay," he said, "But if you need to talk just knock at the door. If I don't answer immediately, don't persist in knocking—it will have to wait until morning." I agreed and said good night. He went into his room and closed the door, and I went downstairs and lay in the big bed, still nervous, trying to calm myself down and get some rest.

After a minute or two I noticed something out of the corner of my eye, off to the right and about five feet in midair. A hole seemed to be opening in space. I rubbed my eyes and shook my head. Taking another careful look, I saw that the hole was definitely getting larger—now it was about two feet in diameter, and still growing. I didn't know whether to believe what I was seeing, even though I was certain that I was awake, not dreaming. I called to the others, but they were all dead to the world, and didn't stir at my voice.

The next thing I knew, a large, beautiful, brownish-gray snake with feather-like glistening scales in a crisp diamond pattern slithered out of the hole and circled around the room at a height of about five feet.

The serpent was about two feet around and thirty-five feet long. I sat there frozen, not knowing what to do. I almost laughed at how absurd the situation was.

From the first moment that the hole appeared, the space of the room began rippling—it didn't seem as if the environment was stable any more, and I recognized that I was watching a change of space taking place in the room.

The room was molding itself into another form. As soon as the snake's eyes emerged from the hole, I heard a voice explaining to me that I should always remember to relate to the universe knowing that it is alive and conscious.

I knew that this was not just ordinary information, but some kind of higher knowledge. I also received other knowledge at that time. It took only a few minutes to transmit a vast body of knowledge that would normally have taken years to communicate in the ordinary way.

All of a sudden I must have kicked back to my normal human consciousness. I found myself wondering if the transcending factor of that experience was going to be that I would be enveloped by the snake. I didn't want that to happen, so I jumped up and ran upstairs.

I didn't look back at the snake as I banged on Mr. Gold's door. He said to come in, and believe me, I did.

"What's the matter, serpent got your tongue?" he asked, laughing heartily and looking at me with the glee of the Joker, straight out of Batman.

I told him what had happened—as if I had to! He just laughed some more, motioning me to sit down on the edge of the bed. He stayed awake with me until morning, talking about techniques for moving through and recognizing different consciousnesses and spaces, and for handling form changes and space changes with certainty and finesse.

I couldn't—and wouldn't—begin to repeat everything he said that night about these things, but I felt that I was reviewing many past experiences of this life and other lives, and seeing this present lifetime in an entirely new perspective.

I finally felt able to get some rest at around five in the morning. I opened the door and peered out over the balcony—just checking! I cautiously tiptoed down the stairs, jumped into bed, pulled the covers over my head—a sure remedy for thirty-five foot floating snakes—and hoped for some good rest. I needed it, after fighting dragons all night.

After two hours of dreamless sleep I got up and had a late breakfast and joined the rest of the students outside. They were doing gardening and ground maintenance work. The regular schedule for waking and cleaning involved getting up before sunrise, and I had missed nearly four hours of work.

"What happened to you?" asked one of the women, as she pulled weeds in the garden.

"I don't want to talk about it," I said as nicely as I could, not knowing whether it was okay to discuss such things among ourselves.

"It's okay," she said. "We just can't talk about things we hear in class."

"Well, I saw a snake," I admitted, hoping she wouldn't laugh. I took myself very seriously at that time.

"Hey," she yelled to the others. "She saw the snake!" "You're going to do okay," she said, as if that explained everything. She showed me how to tell which were weeds and which were the plants deliberately put there, and I helped her until lunchtime, at which time we broke work and gathered on the sundeck where we had a table set up for outdoor meals. We only ate indoors when it was cold or foggy.

After we finished kitchen cleanup we gathered in the main room for movement exercises. I didn't know what we were supposed to do, or what was going to happen, and none of the other students would explain it to me. They told me to just relax, that everything would be explained in its own time.

We all sat in a circle, tailor fashion, and quietly waited. Finally Mr. Gold's door opened and he came downstairs and stood very still in the midde of the circle for a long time, looking at each of us.

When we compared notes later on, it seemed to the group that he had been weighing each of us, and sometimes it felt as if he was looking right through you. We all mutually agreed that we were uncomfortable around him, because we could not seem to hide anything from him successfully. And it was proven time and again that we were right about this.

Mr. Gold motioned us to rise and join hands. He instructed us to keep our eyes open and to look directly into the eyes of the person opposite us in the circle. Then he began to show us the correct steps to do with our feet, and the positions the body should be in while doing what we called our "circle dancing".

The circle began to move slowly around and around. The students were concentrating on forming a deliberate union between the inner exercise he had given us and the outer movement and space around us. Suddenly our hands fused and our arms melted into a pair of tubular arms encircling the group.

An aura of yellowish-white light glowed around the circle, and the whole atmosphere took on that color. A heavy smell of something similar to sulphur filled the air. I had the feeling that it was just my own arms that had elongated around the circle, but as I found out later, everyone had the same impression. From their own point of view they were each the center of this phenomenon.

At that point Mr. Gold must have started to play some music, for I heard sounds flowing in unison with the motion of the circle. The smell returned to its original fragrance of sandalwood.

The circle began to move faster and faster. All I could see was a pair of eyes across this space fixed on my eyes, and a blur of color going around and around in horizontal streaks.

Then one of the students broke from the circle and started turning in the center. The circle quickly joined again and fused as before. After a short while she rejoined the circle and another student spun to the center. This went on until everyone had had a turn in the center.

Then the circle broke as if on command, and everyone began turning. It seemed timeless. One of the most remarkable things that occurred during this exercise was that no one ever bumped into anyone else, although two of the students did fly out the window still turning all the way down, and one person landed in the fireplace with the fire going red-hot. The amazing thing to all of us was that they were not hurt, and they got right back into the exercise as if nothing had happened. We seemed indestructible as long as we kept turning. It was a flawless and continuous action.

After a while a sudden silence occurred. Everything around me became completely motionless, even though I was still turning.

My perception increased to where I was occupying every point existing in that space, and simultaneously experiencing every viewpoint's impression of what was occurring at that time.

Suddenly I became aware that Mr. Gold was playing some music again. The effect of the sounds I was hearing was an incredible shock. I jumped up not knowing where I was and ran outside into the garden. All I could do was cry. I just cried and cried.

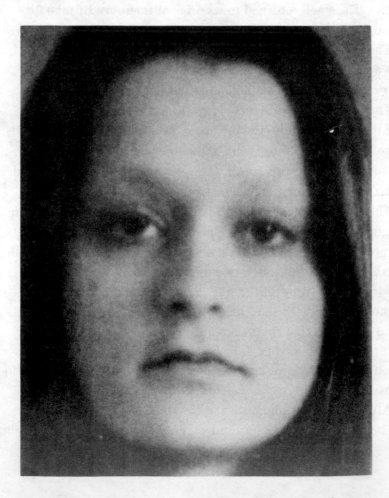

A short while later Mr. Gold came outside into the garden and asked me what was happening. I told him to stay away from me, that I wasn't sure who he was or who I was.

He stayed about eight feet away from me and asked me to describe what I was seeing and how I felt about where I was, and also to tell him what time and place it seemed to be.

I told him that it was June of 1921, of course, and that we were near Paris. I could see Mr. Gold dimly, but he seemed to be somehow different. He had the familiar shaven head and the same piercing but kindly eyes—but his body seemed shorter and thinner.

He said nothing to this but his eyes were asking me not to leave. I told him that I had to go back home, and he said "If you must leave, then you must follow your feelings."

As I described the scene further to him he asked me if I was sure of the time and place. I looked around very carefully and realized that I had been describing something that had happened in the past, and that I was actually outside the Maison Rouge in the San Bernardino mountains of California in the nineteen seventies.

No wonder I was so upset. I had confused this experience with another time in which I had left the school before I could accomplish my work there.

That memory had come back for me to look at and to remember where I had left off last time.

I cried for at least eight hours off and on. It was happening, and I was on the rollercoaster, and there was no letting go until I had gone completely through it.

Thinking now about that experience out there in the garden with Mr. Gold still gives me the chills when I realize that many people have a similar experience, but feel unable to do anything to change it this time.

PROLOGUE

Can it be? Is it possible that my friends and I — who have been arguing for the past half-hour or so about going out of the hotel room — have gotten ourselves once again into that state in which we await rebirth?

Could this hotel — seemingly just an ordinary hotel — actually be the Grand Hotel . . . That place in which we all gather while waiting for the forces of rebirth to catch up to us and push us into a womb, in which we generally sing, yell, dance, wander, party, and in short raise all kinds of hell until that inevitable moment when we utter with a voice filled with surprise and wonder that phrase that signifies to ourselves that the rebirth process has begun? That single-word phrase: "Oops!". . . ?

And all this time I had hoped that I would somehow recognize it and be prepared for it. Why did it get past me again? It now seems so obvious. Here we sit in this room . . . There are six of us remaining, because some have already "gone downstairs" . . . Which I now realize means more than just to "go downstairs"—it means that they have taken rebirth.

Up to now I had thought that this was just an ordinary room party at some convention or other. I never questioned the situation . . . It all appeared to be so ordinary that I never thought to examine it. . . Unless you took everything literally it didn't seem unusual. For instance, when someone said "I'm going to the ballroom," I assumed he meant that he was going dancing . . . And in a way, he was.

But is it too late? No . . . I have not yet felt the tug to go downstairs. This means that I have come to my senses before the process of rebirth has begun. I still have the *chance to do something now, if I act immediately to alter the inevitable chain of events.*

But I had better choose my actions carefully. Everything is so mixed up here. When I think that I am doing one thing, I may be doing something quite different. All my perceptions are wrong. When I believe myself to be in the shower, I am not in the shower at all. I am just seeing it that way.

But where am I in reality? I had better find the answer to this quickly, because here I am now in the shower, and yet I cannot recall having left the hotel room to come here.

Let me take stock of the situation:

I seem to be in a very large bathroom with a great number of toilets and commodes, sinks and showers . . . but no tubs. The floor seems to be tiled and everything is open— with no provision for privacy. Aha . . . There are some others here . . . But they are both male and female, doing these things together . . .

There is no longer any doubt, if there was before. This is definitely the Grand Hotel Rebirth Station in the Third Stage before rebirth, and I had better do something now or I will get caught up in the machine before I can do anything about it. I know that it is already too late to prevent rebirth, but I still have the ability to choose which one I take.

Let's see what else I can observe about this bathroom— perhaps it will give me some idea of what to do.

The floor is filthy, swamped with a mixture of water and something else . . . I hope not what I'm thinking it is.

I can't seem to smell, but if I could I can imagine what it would smell like. The impressions and leavings of billions and trillions of beings who have passed through here on the way to rebirth.

Now I suddenly find myself sitting on the special seat, making a bowel movement. I get the momentary impression that I am giving birth to myself, sending a form down into the material world in which I am soon going to be forced to appear.

If this is true, then I am already on a predetermined path, and there is nothing I can do about it! No . . . I know with at least some part of my being that there are still a few options for me if only I can free myself of these compulsive actions even for one single moment.

I cannot return to the room . . . I know this. There is nothing there for me in any case. But why is it so hard for me to remember what comes next?

I am aware that the hotel is a symbolized projection for what is actually a protective buffering mechanism while my psyche dissolves. But there is something more about this—something painful. What could it be?

Let me see . . . I recall a feeling of vertigo, as if I were being drawn down into a whirlpool. And then there was the thought that I might not ever come out of it, whatever "it" was.

I remember saying "Why, I've lost my mind," as I watched it drift away and dissipate in the Void.

But then what happened? Oh, yes . . . It comes back to me now. A rippling sensation and then a sensation similar to that which must be felt by a body when it is torn apart and quartered. But now that I realize that I am in the between lives state, I see that it could not possibly have been a sensation connected to the body, but that sensation which occurs when the Body of Habits is stripped of its psyche . . . and when the Basic Habits which comprise my eternally surviving Self were taken apart and rearranged during the early stages of this process.

But I did come out of it after all! Here I am . . . Although I must have blacked out just after or during that ordeal.

It is getting later and later. If I am unable to think of something to do to break this compulsive chain of events, I will be drawn into an unconscious rebirth. Why am I so strangely calm about all this? Could it be that I have made arrangements beforehand to automatically choose conscious rebirth? I hope so, because it is becoming more and more obvious that I cannot now change anything while in this state. I will have to depend upon previously ingrained hab-

its—I hope conscious ones—to take "as if conscious action" during this stage in which I am forced to do only in a predetermined way. The machine is set, and I am unable to alter it while I am inside it.

But what is happening now? I am suddenly no longer inside the Grand Hotel. Where am I? Or, more correctly, now that I know that I am in the stage just before rebirth, where do I seem to be?

* * * * *

This cannot be an ordinary theater, even though at first glance it seems to be. Everyone is sitting here watching the screen, but there is no movie being shown. Yet they are all laughing, crying, hoping and feeling all sorts of emotions as if they can see something I cannot. What could they be looking at? Ah, now I am beginning to see it . . . There is an image forming on the screen . . . It seems to be a scene from my former life.

But wait! I do not wish to become caught up in this! I know that the inevitable result of becoming hypnotized by this self-projected scenario will be a completely automatic and mechanical rebirth, and not too far in the future, either, if I allow this to happen to myself. No! I must get away from the theater immediately.

I navigate myself up the aisle and out the door, up the ramp to the street. Something is very odd. There is no traffic out here, and no one walking by. There are only a few buildings, instead of the numerous shops and apartment buildings I expected. I realize that I am looking at the forms of rebirth stations as they are from outside.

I must get home somehow . . . But what is "home", now that I am in this state? I know that I have something that I call home, and that it is possible for me to reach it before the rebirth process takes over completely.

Here is my vehicle. But I cannot drive in this condition. I am dizzy, weak, and confused. Wait . . . Someone seems to be coming toward me. I know this person. He is a friend. And yet I cannot remember how I know him.

Perhaps I am wrong about this. . . Maybe he has come to take me back to the theater. I know that they will not allow me to remain free if they find out I'm gone.

The street is filling with people now. I must get home before they know that I have left the theater.

He wants to get into the car with me, but I have the doors all safely locked. He is saying something, but I must remain free, and cannot take a chance. He says he wants to help me. I can hear him now that I have open-ed the window slightly. I cannot in any case get home by myself—I will have to trust him.

We are moving very slowly . . . I ask him repeatedly if he is sure about the way. He says that he is, and that we will be there very soon. I wish we could go faster, but that would give us away. We must move with the flow of traffic around us.

At last we arrive, and I run inside before my reactions to this give me away. He is just behind me, and soon we are safely protected by the walls of Home.

No one can come in here now and take me back. I will remain free.

But what is happening? I feel as if everything is going to happen all over again. I cannot go through all this again. I am dying . . . and being reborn . . . and dying again and again, over and over. I cannot stand this—it requires so much energy to maintain it and myself.

I must get out of this condition in which every breath is a full lifetime. But I know that if I leave now, I will be forced into a random rebirth. Somehow I must endure all this until I can center myself and choose my path with care and attention.

I look around and see a table—low, black, with white designs on its top—there is a wall partition which cuts the desk area from the rest of the space.

"Nice place we have here," I find myself saying. He nods in agreement as we sit in this safe space called Home.

There are some cards in front of me . . . A deck of Tarot cards. I know that they are somehow special in this space, but I have forgotten just how. . . Perhaps if I alter their relative positions . . . As I do this, something inside myself seems to change in accordance with the change in position of the cards.

Now it seems right. The alteration of the cards has also changed the space, and it is taking on a new form. I seem to be in an old musty bookstore, in which there are many rare books. Maybe some of them can tell me what to do now.

I look at each one, and to my horror discover that they all say the same thing . . . The one thought that I must never think.

Now I find myself in a huge mansion. The walls are painted a light green and the ceiling is very high. There are intricate wood carvings of molding around the tall French doors, which are placed at intervals along the hallway.

I open one, but decide not to enter, in case this is a disguised form of a womb. I cannot now remember how all this is going to happen, but I know that sooner or later I will make a mistake and end up in rebirth.

Inside the room a young lady sits waiting for someone or something. She follows my motion with her eyes as I almost go into the room. She seems unable to move, as if frozen by the sight of me. I go backward and close the door. I do not want to frighten or upset her.

Now I find myself inside a department store . . . But something is very wrong about this place. Everyone is moving up and down on escalators, yet no one seems to be shopping. I decide to see where they are all going, and follow the crowd. As we ride upward I feel a tugging sensation. I look around, but no one else seems to notice it. I realize that this is the first pulling force toward rebirth and jump over the railing. There must be some way to stop this inexorable forward motion long enough to at least take stock of the situation and get my bearings.

I manage to find a stairway and move toward it. Reaching inside my pocket I suddenly discover something and hold it so I can see what it is . . . A black mask. Without really understanding why I do it, I put it on and go onto the closed stairway.

As I walk downward I encounter several others who run from me, shouting "The Black Gang is coming!"

Now I remember. The Black Gang, those whose task it is to frighten beings into rebirth.

Suddenly I realize with a cold chill that I have been descending the staircase for some time now without having seen a landing or a door. I calm my rising panic and stop for a moment. I decide that somehow I am being prevented from seeing the doors although they must be there.

I feel the walls until a door opens. Without actually going through the door I find myself outside upon the greens. I lay down on the grass for a while, relieved to have escaped the department store Rebirth Station.

Again without knowing how I made the transition from the grassy area to this space, I find myself flying low in the air, face upward, feet first.

As I maneuver past telephone poles and wires I think about gaining more altitude. It does not strike me as odd to fly without an airplane. But just as I think about this, I find myself slipping into the passenger compartment of an airplane. Now I am in a seat, along with a number of other passengers.

The airplane begins to lose altitude suddenly, and before anyone can utter a word we crash into the woods below, smashing nose first into a clump of trees.

Suddenly I find myself outside the airplane. I hear the sound of a little girl giggling. I see her dancing through the wreckage, laughing in a combination of tinkling giggles and cackling.

She looks up at me with an expression of amusement. Somehow I know that if she wanted to, she could end it all for me . . . But she won't. She smiles at me and waves hello.

"What's the matter," she asks, "Have you forgotten again?"

I am about to answer, when I suddenly find myself in a small camping trailer. There is someone here with me. He has very long arms and holds onto a railing above him as he talks. I seem to be able to relate to him very easily, and we talk a bit about fear and confusion.

Now I remember how it is in this space. I see the computer in the center of the room and program in some questions about future actions and existence.

Suddenly the other one across the room becomes my own other head, looking into this space from both ends of the universe at the same moment. I feel the sensation of being stretched around the space and have the momentary fear that I will never get out of this one, but after an eternity it lets go, and we are free to walk in the garden.

As we walk over the rows of plants, I recognize below us tiny houses, rivers, lakes and roads. Can it be that this is the world as seen from above? At this thought, everything changes again.

I find myself now in a room in which my transparent body is filled with stars. I can see my outlined form. There are others in the room, and their forms are similar to mine.

"This is the stage just before rebirth," I explain.

"I was wondering," said one.

"You're going to wonder someday if this was all a dream," I continue, "But it isn't."

"Thanks," responds another.

Now I know what is happening, and how to work with it. I am struggling no longer.

FIRST TRANSFORMATION

I am in a mountain cabin. There is a party going on all around in which I take no part and yet in which I participate. There is a horrible crashing sound outside, followed by screams. Everyone rushes outside, to see what happened. I know that they have been tricked into rebirth. I remain quiet and still, waiting.

SECOND TRANSFORMATION

I find myself walking along a red-dirt road in the mountains. It seems to be a construction site, but there are no road graders or heavy machinery. I stop for a moment. There are sounds behind me. In the moonlight I can see a pack of wild dogs coming toward me.

I stand still, remaining calm and quiet. They stop about ten feet away and circle. I do nothing.

THIRD TRANSFORMATION

Now I find myself between some hills, walking toward a railroad car barn. I walk inside, feeling the cool damp darkness around me. I hear something behind me . . . Footsteps. I see an office with its door open, offering the apparency of safety. Recognizing the nature of the open womb, I laugh loudly and the footsteps stop.

FOURTH TRANSFORMATION

I stand in a barnyard between two large buildings. Just across the way is a large barn with a stairway leading up the side. I know that inside this is a Rebirth Drop, from which one falls into a womb. I see a giant bull coming towards me. I laugh, knowing that I cannot be hurt. The bull vanishes, and a giant chicken takes its place.

"Too absurd," I say loudly, "and the lighting effects are off."

The barnyard set dissolves into nothingness for a moment.

FIFTH TRANSFORMATION

I am on a beach. No one has any food. Boats are beached on the sand to my left. In the panic to leave the mainland, boats capsize and smash on the rocks.

Children are placed in boats and sent off into the water while the parents remain behind crying and screaming with fear.

I remain quiet and calm. No one notices me as they battle for a way off the beach.

SIXTH TRANSFORMATION

I am a Slug In Space, turning and twisting this way and that in order to see myself. I cannot stand the sensation of shapelessness. I must do something to alter this.

Within this body I can hear the monks in my cells as they pray and join their will with mine to create a permanent form.

Suddenly I see my other end. On it is a face—my own face. I realize that it has a will of its own, and that it is opposed to my will to take permanent form.

We stare at each other in horror. I remain calm as the creature I have become screams soundlessly. The screams echo into the Void and reverberate, becoming the world.

SEVENTH TRANSFORMATION

We stand here in this classroom, realizing that we are giant telepathic serpents. Snakes. We snake people can read each other's thoughts. We wait for something to change. I know that this will not last long, either.

EIGHTH TRANSFORMATION

We walk out the door toward the central hall in which giant slugs crawl over the walls. I know that this is Grand Central Station and that we must not fall into the Great Hall. I wait quietly for Traveler's Aid to arrive.

NINTH TRANSFORMATION

We are in the little theater. The red velvet chairs are covered with transparent plastic, looking like internal organs in a giant body with blue walls. We are building the cosmic theater, the Matrix of Space.

We walk outside afterwards, down to a restaurent, and drink some water. I feel the clear water go down alive and conscious of its journey through my form. We return upstairs and I stare at the door marked "330". I quiet my hunger as the others eat. Then I am alone once more.

TENTH TRANSFORMATION

We sit here in the playpen, watching the Red and Blue Things hovering just outside.

ELEVENTH TRANSFORMATION

I hold a living, breathing stone in my hand. It pulsates as I hand it to my companions, to show them that it is alive. We move sideways into another reality.

The crystal is pulsing with life, too. We see the stars fixed in it.

Our arms and legs retract as we sit here. The porthole on the wall opens and a moustached man looks in to see how we are doing.

TWELFTH TRANSFORMATION

I am in an apartment in which there is a wooden parquet floor. In the sunken living room there is an orange glow from the cabinet light. I look up and see the audience in the balcony above.

THIRTEENTH TRANSFORMATION

I am almost at the point of rebirth and awakening. It is visible just ahead and I move toward it.

FOURTEENTH TRANSFORMATION

This is the last time I will be human for a while. I feel a momentary pang of regret as I enter the human world, knowing that I will never really be a part of it.

I know that nothing will be lost . . . My sense of wonder is still strong. I relax as I enter the open womb, and allow myself to fall asleep for the last time.

CHAPTER ONE

THE MEETING

It was a cold day in January in the New York City of the nineteen fifties. I had been living in a "by the yearly lease" hotel on Broadway uptown. After stopping in at the delicatessen and bakery on seventy-fourth street I was on my way via subway to a small and virtually unknown restaurant catering primarily to pre-revolution members of the Romanoff family and also was—although this secret was not shared by anyone else that I know of—a gathering place for a certain esoteric brotherhood of unknowable mystics—which said restaurant was called *Alex's Borscht Bowl*—since then defunct.

Thanks to my accidental discovery of the aforementioned esoteric brotherhood which met there, it was for me an ideal starting place on my quest for the *Hidden Guides* who could, according to all reports, lead me to the *Inner World Kingdom,* which I had heard so much about, and had longed to visit.

I knew that it would be difficult to locate the *Hidden Guides,* who are, as everyone knows, the real source of all evolutionary impulses among humanity. After all, if they were easy to find, why would they be called "hidden"?

But when I got to Alex's, it was peopled as usual by— people. They were obviously the same old crowd—if five or six people can be called a "crowd"—of prewar Russian immigrants, who had nothing to do with their time but sit around playing chess all day, and for all I knew, all night as well.

But, on the other hand, I could not help wondering as I sat there quietly in the corner, waiting for the entrance

of some Hidden Guides, who would, I hoped, be wearing
brown or green monks' robes so they could be easily dis-
tinguished from ordinary mortals, whether these quiet
people sitting here every day might perhaps themselves
be . . . But no, according to all logic, it could not be them.

And the reason it could not possibly be them is that if
they were Hidden Guides, they were not out doing their
jobs—that is, *guiding.*

On the other hand, I thought, maybe there is no one to
guide, these days. Maybe no one is interested in the Inner
World any more. Civilization had become so advanced
that, thanks to scientists, doctors, and educators, everyone
already knew where they could go.

But as I sat there pondering all this, twiddling my potato
soup, I noticed that imperceptibly anger had been building
inside myself. Maybe *some* people don't need guiding, but
I did! These lazy Hidden Guides *were shirking, that's all!*

But—could I go up to them and accuse them of goofing
off? Was it prudent of me to walk up to them and scold
them for deserting the universe just to indulge themselves
in chess games and potato soup? Not without knowing the
extent of their powers, I couldn't. They might decide to
cause me to poof out of existence for my impudence!

At that moment, I resolved to make them work at their
tasks—but how could I confront them with their failure to
perform their jobs without endangering myself?

So I resolved at all costs to somehow become as powerful as they, and then come back and confront them! Thus
began my first Real Aim in life—to become as powerful as
the Hidden Guides, and force them to get back to work.

CHAPTER TWO

ON THE ROAD TO POWER

I walked down the North Road into Jerusalem during the holidays, when many pilgrims come into the city, and along the way I met a man I had known from a special kind of club in London. We walked together for a while, and after we entered the city, he asked me to come with him to a certain Father K.'s house, whcrc there was something that might interest me, since I was searching for power equal to that of the Hidden Guides, which I had already mentioned to him in a moment—actually an hour—of indiscretion.

When we arrived, we found the priest in the front yard of the small building in which he had his habitation. We entered with him, and when my eyesight had adjusted to the dim light, I could see plainly that he had been digging under the floor of his little room.

Underneath the floor was a tunnel of stone, which had been exposed by the diggings. And in a niche cut by the original builders of this stone wall there stood an alabaster jar, very finely carved, alongside of which, perfectly undamaged, were several beautiful glass jars, richly patinaed and glistening with iridescent colors, looking as if they had been gold-leafed and then stained with bright purples, reds, greens and blues.

The monk had made this discovery only hours before, and, knowing that my friend from London was curious about such things, had notified him to come to the city and see them.

The monk opened the jar carefully, so as not to damage the contents, if any. As he pried the top off, we could hear the hiss of air and see a puff of dust.

He reached in and—pulled out a copper scroll! This was incredible! The last scrolls similar to this had been found in the nineteen forties, and related to certain esoteric studies of the Sarmoung Brotherhood! Perhaps this could, after all, help me in my quest.

But it was impossible to read, or to unroll it, as it had crystallized over the centuries.

"I will have to take this to the Jerusalem Museum of Antiquities," he said. "But look here, on the jar—this is interesting enough!"

On the outside of the jar, barely scratched into the surface, making it invisible at first glance, was a crudely cut inscription. And if its penmanship were any indication, it had been inscribed by a dying hand. . .although if penmanship is an indication of a dying hand, then high school and college students in America are already dead.

The inscription read, as nearly as I could copy:

ÆSCULAPIO ET *SANITATI*
L. CLODIUS. HERMIPPUS
QUI VIXIT ANNOS CXV. DIES V.
PUELLARUM ANHELITU
QUOD ETIAM POST MORTEM
    EJUS
NON PARUM MIRANTUR PHYSICI
JAM POSTERI SIC VITAM DUCITE

Which tells us that a certain L. Claudius Hermippus lived for one hundred and fifteen years and five days through the breath of young women, which should be worthy of the consideration of physicians and of posterity.

Now, if we take this inscription at face value, it means that a man lived to a very advanced age through some use of the breath of young women. Now, what contribution, I wondered, could the breath of young women make toward maintaining life, and toward extension of the life span?

"Eh, eh," grunted the monk, "What do you make of it?"

"I think that what we have here," said the Londoner, "is a jar temporarily in the possession of an early Western practitioner of the Tantric Tradition, which uses, in its left-hand path, certain esoteric sexual rituals—some of which can be applied to increase the lifespan."

"But what good does that tiny bit of information do?" I asked. "There are no instructions about using or applying it."

When my friend from London, peace be upon him, refused to explain, I believed that it was either because of his own lack of knowledge, or that he was unwilling to discuss anything relating to sex because of my age.

Now that I think about this incident, however, I realize that he communicated no other information about this to me not because he knew nothing about it, or because of my young age, but because this kind of information must be personally elucidated for oneself through intentional efforts. Besides which, I could not at that time put these things into practice, and therefore had no immediate use for them. When they became necessary, as with every piece of knowledge I have received, they were available to me.

The only things he would discuss with me at that time were the two things I was interested in: the existence of entrances to the Inner World Kingdom, and the Hidden Guides, who occasionally come to the surface world in order to provide the source material for the formation of conscious life in certain members of the human community who have, as a result of a combination of efforts of a very special kind, and sheer chance, become as is said, "Candidates For Another Life".

It might be of use to others to pass on some of the things he mentioned that day about the Inner World Kingdom—its construction, language, and the presence of entrances to it, which—although now closed due to the overenthusiasm of several violence-loving participants of several martial conflicts including the Second World War, The Great War, The Crimean War, and The Moldavian Conflict, could be opened with right effort and right knowledge.

I was eager to learn in the short time allowed for it, the methods possessed by him for opening the Inner World doorways, called "gateways".

Somehow I managed without a tape recorder or notes, to retain almost verbatim all the data presented by him on the subject, perhaps as a result of the ingestion of "mastique" and peta bread sandwiches which he called "Turkish Tacos" all this became associated with something pleasant, and was assimilated in my most deeply rooted consciousness.

It was lucky in one respect that I was able to fully assimilate this data just by hearing it, because only months afterward, my friend from London—peace be upon him— was struck with a bullet during one of the usual urgent crazes among the populace to destroy everything in sight, and he was instantly killed.

But here in essence is what he managed to transmit to me before that occurred:

There is an enormous pile of rubbish heaped up on the entrances to the Inner World, thanks to man's unconscious manifestations in the outer world, and only a very disturbed person, or one greatly in need, would consider trying to clear the passage—moreover someone not only disturbed, but used to hard labour and willing to expend much energy without knowing for certain what may ultimately come of it.

It is the custom of ordinary man to block up these entrances if found, and to destroy anyone likely to indicate its whereabouts to others.

Ordinary man fears Inner World Man, and imagines that they steal their children, sour their milk, and destroy crops, as well as other petty mischief. That is to say, rather than see the ordinary manifestations of nature at work, ordinary man seeks vengeance—and finds a harmless scapegoat in Inner World Man, who has found the real meaning and significance of life. Such Real Men represent to them all the things they could be, if not for their negative factors and fears.

*It is rare for someone to find an Inner World entrance
without help of some kind—even if invisible to him—and
we are all guided by a series of seemingly accidental coincidences, and by chance.*

*However, it is possible that the path becomes clearly
marked to an individual who has had his inner sight opened sufficiently to see the markings, ravaged though they
may be by the passage of time and the destructive urges
of wild animals, not the least of which is the arch-destroy-
er of all time, "man".*

*And even if one gains access to the Inner World, there
is still the matter of earning one's livelihood. One must
be familiar with ordinary hand-crafts, particularly the repair variety, without the loss of self-respect as a result of
engaging in menial tasks decidedly not the essence of ordinary dignity as understood by modern man.*

*This is all necessary, for no one has "powers" in the
Inner World Kingdom—all powers must be given up to
another specific individual.* (Note: more will be said
about this in a later discourse)

*Contrary to the beliefs currently held by modern man
about the Inner World inhabitants—if indeed anything
has survived at all, through the widespread assumption
that Inner World inhabitants simply sit about, staring at
clouds—the real Inner World inhabitants must at all
times live by their wits—tempered by their conscience—
not only in the Inner World Kingdom, but also when
going into the outer world among humans.*

*Living by one's wits is only attained and mastered as
an art through long apprenticeship.*

*Occasionally a few Inner World inhabitants come into
the outer world in which man now reigns supreme, unfortunately, thanks to his willingness to destroy not only other beings, but even those similar to himself.*

*These Inner World inhabitants sometimes come to
enact certain steps which have become necessary due
to man's insistence on destroying not only himself, which
would be a blessing, but also the planet, in his headlong
rush into oblivion.*

The unconscious manifestations of outer world beings, particularly humans, inevitably draws off certain types of Inner World energy which cannot be replaced. This occurs largely because they employ labour-saving devices to save themselves some of their precious time.

They only do this because of an inherent pattern of laziness and tendencies to allow machines to perform labours for them—labor that rightfully belongs to the essence. And considering the quality of their thought reproductions—not at all intentionally aroused in them—this may be not at all a "bad thing".

And so this destructive population of men, called by Inner World inhabitants "Outhabitants" as a giggle, have for centuries believed that they must at all costs allow all unconscious urges of theirs to manifest, especially those which dictate survival, regardless of the damage it causes to others, and to the Inner World, without which they could not possibly survive even one day, and about which they have conveniently forgotten.

Not only are they unaware of the results of these unconscious urges of theirs, but they are completely unaware of the urges themselves—they literally have no idea of what they are doing!

But in the Inner World, things are different. There, everyone is aware of the totality of effects in the world of action, and therefore all actions are taken with direct knowledge of their results.

None of the Outhabitants of the world have by themselves enough power to draw off very much Inner World energy, but the combined action of unconscious beings is more than enough to draw off quite a bit of it.

As it is now, this valuable energy usable otherwise for the benefit of all life on the planet—and in some cases elsewhere also—is scattered out into deep space, where it is captured and eaten by certain blue beings and their consorts who exist on the outermost limits of the universe.

The extreme cold and exposure to outer space of the planet earth makes it possible for this Inner World energy which is called "ehiari" to be released into outer space by the process of radiation.

In this way, the human population of earth has stripped the planet of almost all remaining energy needed for further evolution, not only of their own species, but also of all other species on earth, with the singular exception of the cockroach, which will soon be the sole survivor just as it is on the planet Toolikosios, called by humans the planet Mars.

And unfortunately for the few surface dwellers who have—thanks to "chance interventions" of certain Inner World inhabitants who have come to their aid through the enactment of almost i-m-p-e-r-c-e-p-t-i-b-l-e coincidences—a definite possibility of reaching the Inner World through one of the entrances, there are other surface dwellers who wish only to prevent this from occurring, due to fears that others might find happiness and peace, which thanks to their suspicious natures and envious way of life, cannot possibly happen for them unless they gave up everything, which they would never do.

Not only do those perverted beings restrict others in their search for the Inner World, but they force them to slave for the "business commonwealth" by serving in useless occupations which, although serving no real purpose, prevent them from going on the quest for the Inner World.

It is only with conscious help from an Inner World guide that any slave who has become caught up in this gigantic and inexorable machine has any hope of living long enough to find the Inner World entrances, since the power-possessing outer world beings hold "Life-Necessities" as entrapments to hold them in slavery.

Certain definite skills and abilities not normally present in the life of ordinary man must be established if one hopes to become a permanent inhabitant of the Inner World.

Of course without these essential skills one may visit briefly the Inner World, even in frequent intervals. But in order to become a permanent resident—a member of this most exclusive inner circle of humanity, one must develop consciously and intentionally the required skills and attitudes.

At first—and this is the Great Secret—one must make a model of the Inner World, as one conceives it presently. Then one must learn to live in it. That is to say, one is expected to "wring the secrets out of it" before one has actually experienced the Inner World.

One must live as if actually in the Inner World, even though at first it is entirely imaginary. Fortunately, man has within him such a highly developed imagination anyhow, that it will not be hard to imagine oneself as having already fully developed one's abilities as a being, already accepted as one of the brothers or sisters of the highest brotherhoods existing anywhere in the Great Cosmos.

One should imagine oneself to be in a room which is large enough to accomodate oneself and those with whom one wishes to share this room—those one would not mind having close to one in the Inner World for some time— perhaps forever.

One strives to know oneself completely, and to know others with whom one shares this room just as completely. One should try to know others in their being, because once built and occupied, this room, even though purely imaginary, cannot be easily dismantled except afterwards, when one has attained genuine essence.

You may already have guessed that I have not fully reported these instructions for the creation of this room— especially in connection with this incredible idea of utilizing the faculty of imagination—but I will explain all about this startling idea later on in the course of my writings.

CHAPTER THREE

JOURNEY TO OUTAT-EL-HADJ

I left Jerusalem and according to instructions, boarded
a plane for Lisbon, then by car, to boat, and again by car,
to Outat-El-Hadj in Morocco. There I joined up with a
small group of people who had almost the same purpose
as I—to locate the entrance to the Inner World.

Since we were traveling incognito—the absolute best
possible arrangement for Americans overseas—we decided
to call our little group "Sneakers After Truth".

We headed south toward Cairo, and then out into the
Libyan Desert. Our guide, who had been supplied by my
friend from London, allowed us tenderfeet to stop quite
frequently in order to refresh ourselves. One one picnic,
we sat directly on what our guide told us had been an Inner World entrance. We discovered it by accident when
Mr. F. fell into the opening up to his knees.

We quickly enlarged the opening, after pulling him out
of there, using the combination picks and shovels we had
gotten at surplus stores in the States. We were about to
just jump down there, and shimmy down "chimney fashion", when an inner voice cautioned me to be careful.

I insisted that we make a rope out of a number of items
of clothes—none of them my own, of course—but the ama-
teur knots failed, and Mr. F. slipped and fell down into the
hole.

While the others were still engaged in getting him out of
there, I decided to make for the nearest dried prune market, which was at Wadi Seil Fejr, and so I left in the smaller of the three jeeps; as it turned out, it wasn't an Inner

World entrance after all, and many of the group left for
"rope training" exercises in *Rive Gauche,* with a Colonel
Renard—not to get experience in climbing and spelunker-
ing, but because the food was better.

Meanwhile, I had gone on to Smyrna with the guide,
and some of the group came on afterward. We went from
there to Tiflis, and then along the road on the coast to
the east, where we met our next guide who was familiar
with the entrances available in that area. So we said goodbye to our first guide, and were soon well on our way to
discovery of the ancient landmarks signifying entrance-
ways to the Inner World.

CHAPTER FOUR

THE LITTLE HUT IN THE DESERT

At sunset on the first day with our new guide, we arrived
at a new level of land, similar to the cobblestone streets of
New Orleans—but in this case created out of hard volcanic
rock, in natural block formations.

We moved with the stars as our beacons, the Land Rover
running smoothly over the natural basalt roadway. The
blackness of the stone swallowed what little starlight reached it.

At last we stopped, in a gently swept sand-filled valley,
or "wadi". Around us were a few thickets. We gathered
these thorny dry bushes and made a heap of them, which
looked like a pile of snakes.

I fell asleep after the marshmallows, and so missed the
singing which ended at about midnight. In the morning,
at around eleven—which was morning to us—we broke our
fast with some light lunch—peanut butter and jelly sandwiches and lemonade. There was something strangely home-
like and comforting about eating peanut butter and jelly
sandwiches and drinking lemonade out there.

At about four that afternoon, we came to a network of
watershed. The land lay in great swatches of color. I imagined that if I could tell North from South, I could follow
it like a map.

I tried to remember a trick I had learned about determining direction from the flow of sand and the moss on trees,
but it's like "feed a cold and starve a fever. . .or is it starve
a cold and feed a fever?" You see? Nobody really knows.

Finally we arrived at a little hut made of sun-baked
bricks, very much like a sod hut in the American plains.
It was inhabited by a former city-dweller from Sochi—
a Georgian. He entertained us with beautiful songs,
both work songs and sacred songs, which our guide knew,
and accompanied him on a harmonium.

The Georgian had built his hut directly above an entrance to the Inner World—the one we had been searching
for. Our guide was obviously dismayed to find the hut
occupied.

The well inside the house was in fact the entrance and
had been sealed for over six centuries, he said. It had at
some time become blocked by a cave-in of stones, and
had filled with water from that time on to the present.

Of course, had we broken through, the man would have
lost his all-important well, the source of his water. We decided that under no circumstances could we even ask him
permission to do such a thing. Not only would he lose
his source of water, but plants and animals who were also
dependent upon it would inevitably suffer.

When we told our decision to our guide, and stated our
intention to go on to another entrance instead, he smiled
and said, "Very good. You pass the first test of compassion." We had no idea what he was talking about at that
time.

We said our goodbyes to the man in the hut—and our
guide gave certain indications that he had known him for
a lot longer than just the one day.

We continued on our way. Now we went toward Ankara. Most of us had assumed before we went on this journey that we would be deep inside the Inner World by this
time, and some of the group were beginning to run out of
patience and capital. I decided to remain in Ankara for a
while, where I was assured work in my special trades, but
the rest of the group decided to go on to Geneva, where
we had heard of still another Inner World entrance.

This accidental stopover, occuring quite by chance, gave me a unique opportunity which would otherwise have completely passed me by.

As I wandered along the narrow streets trying my hardest "not to be an American", I chanced upon a doorway of what I at first assumed was a carpet shop. Walking through, I discovered that I had blundered into a long narrow hallway, which was very dark except for a few bare lightbulbs hanging from barely covered wires. The lights didn't help much, and my eyes adjusted very slowly to the darker environment.

I assumed that the shop was in back, so I continued to go deeper into the hallway—I suddenly found myself standing in a large foyer in back of which was an enormous room, dimly lighted with hanging lamps of tin or copper, cut to look like the intricate screen work of a mosque or tomb.

In this room were a group of people in strange white costumes, standing around poles jutting up from the floor, in frozen postures which did not change as long as I watched.

A man dressed in ordinary street clothes motioned for me to sit down and remain silent, which I did. I sat there for several hours observing this scene, while the "dancers"—I had already decided that this was some form of dance—moved not even one tenth of an inch. I found myself holding my breath a lot, and had to remind myself to breathe every so often.

I remember thinking that I had better get out of there and that I had obviously stumbled on something usually kept hidden from prying eyes. I was terrified that they would find out that I was not Moslem . . . Yet for some reason I felt compelled to remain there until the "dance" was finished, as I had been told to do.

Finally the group broke and left through a side door. The man in the suit came up to me and now I could see how incredibly tiny and frail he was. I asked him what it was I had wandered into.

"This is called the *Dancing Brotherhood of Honey*," he replied. "But you did not wander. Your friend from London has been shot."

"My God, is he going to be all right?" I asked in shock.

"Oh, yes, quite all right. He died this morning."

At the time it did not occur to me to ask him how he knew me or how he knew my friend from London. Nor did I think to ask how I had come to this place without help of any kind. At that time, if I could not perceive help, it did not exist for me.

We talked for some time, during which I learned that I had been "invited"—in some way unfathomable by me and by my senses or brain—to attend a meeting of an ancient brotherhood which specialized in the keeping of certain insects called by them *moulichik,* which we Americans call "bees".

"But what were they doing in frozen postures?" I asked, realizing that he might not choose to answer, nor was he constrained to give me any explanation. But I hoped and wished to know.

"They were not "frozen," as you say. It is called the *Dance of One Hundred Steps.* Each step requires one thousand years to complete. It is a slow dance, but with practice one can see it from beginning to end."

"But why were they all in different postures?" I asked.

"Each posture is set by the step before it. The dancer may spend years finding the exact posture as it is now in this time. When he assumes the precise position in the dance he sees the entire pageant—all hundred steps. In this way the present, past and future are seen to be one."

"Oh," I replied, at a complete loss. "How do they find the right posture?"

"They hold these ivory hands, connected to jointed arms, which in turn are connected to these center posts," he explained as we examined one of the apparatuses. "In each of these eighteen posts is the secret of all hundred steps. The joints of the arms and hands are set according to this wheel—as you can see, it has several possible settings corresponding to different letters. Thus not only is the dance transmitted, but also an entire set of teachings, contained in aphorisms, passed on through the medium of the experience of timelessness but also through postures determined by the settings of these posts."

CHAPTER FIVE

NEW INSTRUCTIONS

Early next morning I sat outside the foyer, hoping to be invited in. After waiting for several hours, I decided to try the door to the large meeting room, even though it was not open, as it had stood the day before. I felt that if I did not take chances now, I might lose the struggle completely.

There was no one in the back room—it was empty save for the hanging lanterns, which were unlit but just visible by the light of the low-wattage bulbs in the hall. I almost jumped out of my skin at the sight of a figure in the doorway. I had heard nothing of any movement behind me.

It was the same small gentleman I had met the day before.

"This is not for you," he said. "They have gone somewhere else, but in any case, you must be somewhere else now yourself. I will introduce you to someone who can help you find a gateway to the Inner World."

"Where are we going?" I asked him.

"We are not going anywhere together, except at this moment. . .but I will introduce you just the same." He touched my forehead with his fingers, and told me to leave.

"Wander in the market," he said. "Follow your heart. If it leads you rightly, you will have your meeting. And if not, then go home. . . it is not for you yet."

I wandered in the market all day, but nothing struck me, and no one came up to me. I was expecting something unusual to happen—and I thought that it would be best to remain passive and allow whomever it was that was supposed to meet me there to search me out and introduce themselves.

At last, I gave up, and went to find something to eat and drink. It suddenly struck me to order something they could not possibly have, just for the fun of it.

"Je voudrais un'Armagnac," I told the waiter. It was a drink for which I had no taste, but which was just exotic enough to be impossible. I had as my second choice another equally impossible one—Heineken's beer.

"Pardon, said you that you wished Armagnac?" said a voice behind me. I turned to see an older man, semitic, standing behind me. "They have no such thing here, sir," he said with a musical lilt to his voice. The tone seemed almost ingratiating, but it had a quality of humor and life behind it that made it all right for me.

"I know. . .I never expected them to have it," I said.

"Then why did you order it?"

"I don't know—just for a joke, I guess."

I hoped that he would announce something like "Aha, my young friend—I have arrived, and you are invited to a secret meeting!"

But no such conversation took place. He sat down next to me, and I drank some coffee as we talked, mostly about the current political situation. After several hours of this, I excused myself and began wandering in the market again.

I was not doing a very good job of pretending to be European. . . lots of people constantly threw goods in my face. I eventually figured out that it was the camera hanging around my neck that gave me away, but I didn't want to miss any good shots.

Late that evening, I gave up completely and went back to my hotel. At the hotel there was a message to return to the cafe—the one where I had met the elderly gentleman. I was intrigued by all this intrigue, and went, thinking that I must have been on the right track after all, and that he was being coy.

When I got there, the old man was waiting. He explained that he was a magician of the Arabic School—the forerunners of the medieval western alchemists. He had spent a great many years conjuring and classifying demons, efrit, djinn, and astral spirits—classifying them according to height, age, weight, color, size of eyes, facial and body characteristics, attitudes, beliefs, and so forth, including any noms de plume they might have taken through the centuries . . . and in this process he had formulated the exact laws by which the names change—a very important set of laws, for without the exact name, one cannot conjure or evoke a djinn.

"You come to my home, and I show you how to call the djinn," he said. "Someday maybe I show you how to create real outside *debil.*"

"Why would I ever want to know how to do that?" I asked, in some astonishment, and not a little fear that he might be involved in some kind of devil worship cult.

"Someday you wish for *real outside enemy*—not just imaginary force of negative arisings. After you gain powers, you either know how to do this, or you endure living death forever. You find out later, then you wish to know how, and I show you."

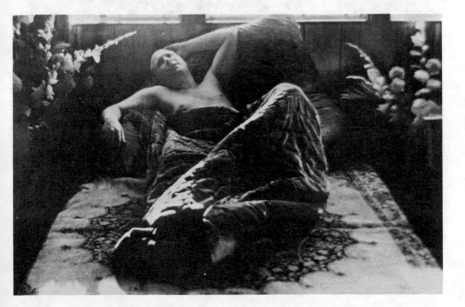

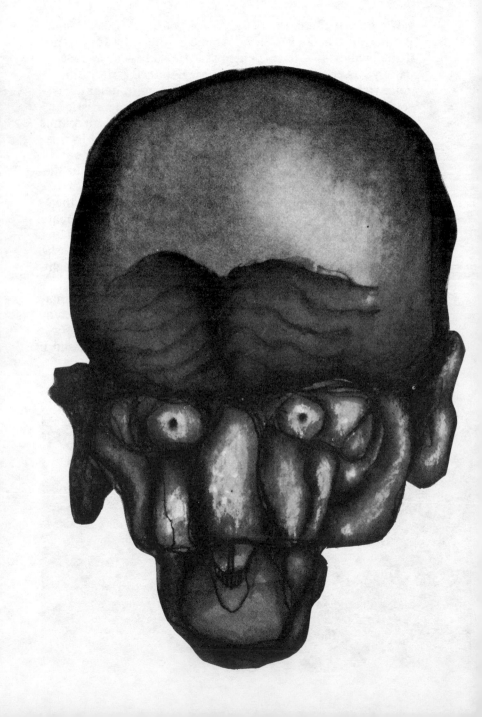

CHAPTER SIX

AT THE MAGICIAN'S HOUSE

I recognized the stench of sulphur and storax the moment I walked into the house. A young man—obviously a house-boy—showed me through a thin veil at the doorway. He stood very quietly when the magician entered, and then he left silently.

The room was not part of regular living quarters. The rest of the house may have had living space . . . I don't know. But this was set up so completely and permanently as a ritual space that I knew it had no other purpose, nor had it been used for any other purpose for some time now.

In one corner was a large cage—almost a compound—in which sat a huskily breathing leopard.

I was shown where to stand during the invocation, and then told by gesture to sit down where I was and not move out of the circled area.

I did not have to be told that! I knew a little of what to expect from my readings on the subject of conjuration. As for anything else beyond the ritual itself, I was prepared to believe only my senses.

I will not bore the reader with the details—it was in all ways usual, except for the sharing of wine, which the magician called *toasting*—and the Method of calling or invoking the Djinn and Efrit, which he called *hoqepatuniun,* or in english, *Stepping On Tender Corns To See What Happens.*

One djinn appeared in a puff of smoke through which we could not see him at first. Finally the smoke cleared, and we could see his huge eyes, small ears, and big mouth.

He stood well over two feet tall and was pretty much a run of the mill demon.

This djinn's brilliance was only exceeded by his stupidity. What the magician got out of evoking a parade of these dull brutes was beyond my comprehension. Oh, I have to admit that I was impressed by the fact that it was possible to conjure them—who wouldn't be impressed by that? But as I soon found out, these unfortunate idiots had not even the slightest degree of reason.

And there is a definite reason for this. A djinn is composed completely of automatic and mechanical habits. Humans, on the other hand, are lucky enough to have the inner being, which is also a collection of mechanical habits, tempered by an outer influence, called the *psyche*. This makes it possible for a human being—unless under stress—to behave more or less with reason and conscience.

But djinn are forced to live in the lower worlds, where the formation of a psyche is impossible. And the lower the djinn world, the less ability to create for oneself any real and stable aim.

Each level of djinn existence is at odds with all other levels. As one djinn takes an action in one world, all other djinn corresponding to that djinn take exactly the same action, as if they were images in a hall of mirrors.

As one takes initiative in its turn, the others become completely passive until the action is completed—or as is more usually the case, until just before it would have been completed, which is a weak point of power, which allows another djinn to take over and change the direction of the intention. Thus no action taken by a djinn can ever be completed. They compete with each other for control, and so the organism in which they all share responsibility and existence is hopelessly doomed to an existence in a circular or square system—and sometimes in a zig-zag or straight-line system—without an end in sight.

The djinn, meanwhile, who are unable to think or to reason, flop about like fish out of water—crying aloud the agony of the results of mechanical action and reaction.

These poor unfortunate habitual beings feel that they are just on the verge of thinking a thought—some thought, any thought—perhaps of some way to escape this perpetual suffering. But just like Tantalus and the grapes, the potential for thinking is just out of reach.

This continual torture of theirs enrages them, causing each of them to lose control, thus allowing the next lower and still lower and lower djinn to take command—until the organism is reduced to a quivering and confused blob of conflicting intentions, commands, and urgent desires, and finally it comes to a complete standstill. Then the whole thing starts over again.

Each of the djinn is completely unaware of the existence and power of the others. Thus, each one believes itself to be the only source of thought, action, and knowledge. The others, if they are noticed at all, are simply thought to be mirror images of the Prime Source.

They cannot conceive of others as entities in their own right—only as reflections of themselves. Each one believes that he and he alone is responsible for his actions, that he guides his own destiny, and that he has the ability to think and to reason, and that he has within himself—without any conscious effort on his part—the possibility of life after ordinary life.

He also believes himself to have—without a shred of doubt—an already established and developed *soul*. It is the existence of such peculiar and fantastic beliefs that separates him from real man.

He is continually confounded by the seeming variations in his plans. He cannot understand why his best-laid plans go completely into other directions. This is because he cannot see the actions of other djinn as they take control and begin to force the organism to do their bidding according to their own intentions and desires.

The names of these djinn continually change. They will not appear twice under the same name, and so the magician must be aware of the new form in which they will manifest. If he calls the wrong name, they are not compelled to appear. This is called the *Law of Ifritic Conjuration*.

The entire process of conjuration has been lost to the new generations of man, of course, due to confusion about what it is, and what it is used for. This was no accident.

During the period called the Middle Ages, there was a break in the tensions between worlds that normally keeps them separate. In this short interval, hundreds of djinn and ifrits managed to climb through the gap, and shortly took up residence in the human world.

Finding that the humans were subject to outer influence, and were easily subjugated through fear and willingness to believe even the most preposterous of ideas, they fed the vivid imaginations of humans with tales of demons, fires of hell, and devilish witchcraft. They told the humans that there were evil things all around them, and that the only solution to this was to allow the djinn to protect them.

The humans, of course, were so filled with gratitude that they instantly made the djinn heads of state, church, and education. The djinn, to protect themselves, forbade the use or study of conjuration—had this knowledge been allowed, the humans would have eventually come to know the origin of these creatures, and could have sent them back where they came from.

By now, of course, since these creatures have had their way for so long, humans have even forgotten what the word conjuration means. They think it means to raise the dead or something equally absurd, when in fact it simply means *con,* from the Latin, *with;* and *jure,* also from Latin, meaning *knowledge* or *understanding.* So conjure means, quite simply, *with knowledge.*

Thanks to these power-possessing djinn now in control of the world of humans, many such words have been lost to meaning—such as the word *seance,* which means "to sit very quietly".

How then does a magician know which djinn to call at any given moment? How does he know which djinn, out of millions of possible causes, is responsible for the organism's current state of action, thoughts and beliefs?

At the exact moment that a djinn takes over the actions of the organism, he lights up—just like a beacon—thus enabling the magician to recognize him and to correctly call his name.

For example, if the djinn currently in charge was the type that tries to attain a goal by oblique or indirect action, he would be called in the list of *zig-zag djinn*. If, on the other hand, he were the type of djinn that tries to achieve things by taking no action whatever, and remaining perfectly still, he would be found listed under the heading of *point-djinn*.

If these djinn did not, while they are initiating action, announce themselves and demand that they be recognized as the permanent and rightful masters of the organism, they would probably never get caught. But their strident insistence on recognition gives them away every time. This science of recognition and naming of djinn is called, in the tradition, *The Science of Masks*, or in the language of magicians, *Le Science du Idiote*.

After the ritual had been completed, we sat in the other end of the living room, and had some herbal tea—mint, I think. I was told that I could now ask any questions that I wished to. Did I have any questions? You bet I did!

But unfortunately, the magician, who was tired and exhausted from all that effort, fell promptly asleep.

So I left the house, nodding good night to the houseboy, and also, just in case we met again under other circumstances, to the leopard.

Then, meandering in a more or less purposeless way, as I was wound up to a high pitch of excitement as a result of all this, and it would have been impossible for me to sleep at that time, I wandered along the streets in the semi-darkness of pre-dawn.

Guide #2   E.J. Gold '76

CHAPTER SEVEN

WANDERINGS

Some of the shopkeepers were already putting up their
stalls, and the inert interiors of the permanent indoor shops
still remained silent and empty. The living quarters above
the stores were dark except for a few lights in one window,
and then in another, farther down the block.

The merchants from the indoor shops did not have to
set their shops up every day, as did the outdoor merchants.
As I walked, and watched such ordinary, everyday activity,
it became harder and harder to believe what I had witnessed
earlier.

But all of a sudden, as I turned a corner, I saw one of the
djinn from the magician's conjurations. Then, one by one,
I saw many other djinn appearing on the street. They proceeded to set up shop just as if they were ordinary humans.
They recognized me, also, because as I passed, they nodded
to me, as if to say, "Yes, it's me . . . but you had better not
alert the human populace about this, if you wish to spend
the rest of your allotted days on earth rather than in the
ghost world."

I began to hum a little tune as I walked, to show that I
was not afraid of them. Suddenly I realized that it was a
tune that I had heard at the dancers. I had seen something
astounding just now, which was, at least in my subconscious
mentation, associated in some way with the strange motionless "dance" of the group I had seen in the room at the back
of the narrow, dimly lit hallway.

I began to wonder whether I might have made a mistake by not going on with the group searching for Inner World entrances, but there began to form in me at this time some indefinable urge which made me feel as if something was happening that was exactly what was needed to shock my inner world to life.

The very real question of choosing between these two possible courses of action began to attain a terrible importance. I had to know which of these was real.

It was a frightening thought, which suddenly struck me as I walked through the streets, that neither of them might be real. Up to that moment, I had thought that at least one of them must be. But that would have negated all my previous work, so I stuck with my original thesis that both of them were equally real, but that one course of action might be more suited to my needs than the other.

The observation of the magician, and the mysterious motionless dance of the men who met in the room back of the hallway, the keepers of bees, were far stronger calls to my essence—and no doubt also to my psyche—than the prospect of digging around, grubbing through garbage and caves to get to the Inner World.

I was on my own, however, without a guide, in a country whose language I did not speak, and whose customs I was totally ignorant about. Yet it seemed to me that I was at home, for the first time in my life.

In the thinking and feeling process which had become aroused in me as a result of the spectacular demonstration at the magician's, there began to appear a new kind of feeling—a sort of attention, in which I could now suddenly perceive all at once everything that was happening in my mind, body, and emotions. I decided, without knowing what else to call it, to name this new feeling *a complete sensing of myself.*

Along with this, there appeared to be an unusual accompanying state, in which I seemed to be as light as a feather—no, lighter than air. I felt as though everything around me had become existent in a new way—visible, but solid only in the mind, and not in space or time. I decided to call this other new state, a state of *impersonal attention and aware-*

ness. I later learned that this state is also called *interested cosmic indifference.*

It was at this moment that I understood what is meant when it is said that cosmic love is completely impartial, and that love is not something projected onto others, or held, or received, but is the very essence of one—one cannot love, or be loved, but can *be love itself.* To me, love became an entity within which one can exist continually.

I realized, after some time, that I was nowhere near my hotel, and even though the streets were unfamiliar to me, I refused—because I did not wish to interrupt my new state—to ask directions of anyone.

And so it was not until after dark that I arrived at my hotel. There was a note waiting from me. It said that I was invited to attend a meeting of the "Dancing Brotherhood of Honey" that afternoon, and not to be late. But it was already evening. I had missed them!

I quickly broke my state, and set off as fast as I could in the right direction, not allowing the former state to interfere in my ability to choose direction, as I had before. But when I got to the building, the room was again locked.

Not only had I missed them for that day, but when I returned the next day and waited in vain until the evening at five o'clock—you can always tell when it is five o' clock there—I realized that I might have missed them for good.

Day after day I sat outside the hallway, and day after day no one came. I was going through all this hardship and misery simply because I had not wanted to break my new state. I had fallen in love with a state of being! That was the reason I had not asked directions, and had I allowed the state to dissipate, I could have been here in time.

In the end I returned to my hotel room after three profitless days sitting in front of the building near the marketplace.

I walked the room like a madman, around and around the little room, navigating the furniture, scuffling over the worn ragtag carpet, paying little attention to the bare furnishings and "early Woolworth" prints hanging on the walls. Besides the skimpy furnishings, there was a pink-striped wallpaper on all the walls, and the bed sagged dangerously.

I paced up and down, back and forth, huffing and puffing, trying to catch my breath, which seemed to be always one step ahead of me. I mentally beat myself for being such an egoist and lover of my own temporary and extremely transitory states. How could I have been so stupid? How could I have allowed my curiosity about a trifle to overcome me so much that I lost everything? How could I have betrayed my inner aim for nothing?

After a while of this—it could have been several hours or only a few minutes; I have no way of knowing—it suddenly came to me that at least, according to my behavior and probably according also to my inner state of loss and importance, I had *i-m-p-e-r-c-e-p-t-i-b-l-y* become a djinn!

Somehow I managed to leave the hotel—or more correctly, to persuade the djinn in charge of my organism to leave it—and make my way to the street, and eventually to the magician's house. I hoped he could help me regain myself, because at this point, all I could do was to helplessly watch myself enacting the various—and conflicting—commands of any djinn that happened to be in control of my body.

How I found his house in the midst of this state—or series of states—is still amazing to me. In all this self-pity and self-flagellation I had lost the conscious memory of its location. But something inside guided me directly to it.

It became clear to me afterwards that there must be a certain "something" inside which is not part of the normal everyday consciousness, which could think and act without my intentional direction.

I had discovered the independent thinking and acting mind which operates only when the ordinary mind is out of action and control. The house of the eighteen djinn.

As I arrived at the door, I was let inside not by the house-boy, but by one of the motionless dancers of the Brotherhood of Honey. It was suddenly obvious to me that this man I had met by chance in the marketplace was in reality not a magician at all, nor was my meeting with him complete chance as I had imagined. Here was the Brotherhood of The Inner World. In one motion, I had found my guide, and I had discovered—or been led to—an entrance to the Inner World.

40) ALIENS AMONG US, 1976   8"x10"

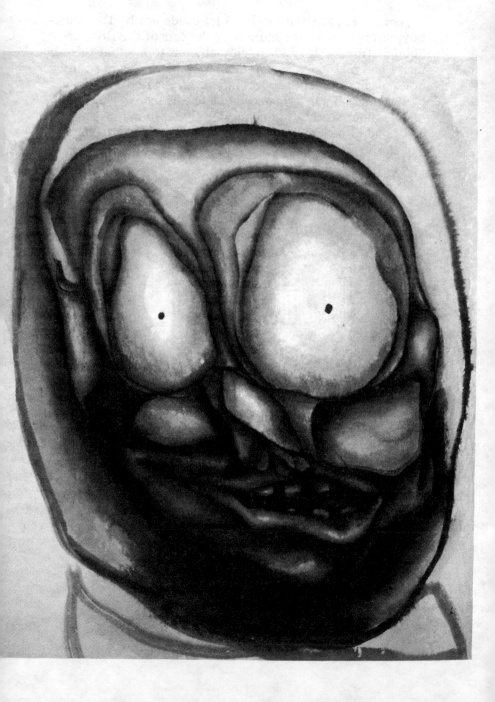

CHAPTER EIGHT

SANITY AT LAST

Even in my wildest fantasies I could not have imagined such an outcome. Here I stood, among the members of the Inner World Brotherhood—and I had been foolish enough the previous visit to believe completely and without question that I had been witnessing the manifestations of djinn, when in fact it was only a few tricks mixed with a few real things.

They must have followed me after I left, and knowing that I could not possibly arrive at the hotel until late, put that message in my mailbox just as a joke, realizing that I would get into a full-blown panic over having missed them.

But, now I must apologize, dear reader, for doing it once again. I have taken us off on still another flight of fancy—into the daydreams of yesterday. But yesterday is not today, and we wish to know what took place at Alex's Borscht Bowl. I will try not to stretch your credulity again, recognizing that only so much of this "stuff and nonsense can be tolerated by a serious seeker after truth. And so I will try to confine my remarks only to those incidents which occurred at Alex's Borscht Bowl on that cold January day in 1955.

However, I have no doubt that this mental wandering of mine more or less matches your own tendency to wander "ever so slightly" away from the object of your attention, and so you should not complain. . . not even whimper.

You should have realized by now that this astral travel of ours through Turkey and Geneva and Spain and all of the equally fascinating and exotic countries we could float into will get us nowhere in a real way. This wandering occurs, as you are doubtless aware, only in a being in whom no real center of gravity has formed, and in which there has not been actualized the knowledge of how serious it all is. In short, this could only happen to a being who had accidentally or deliberately formed a "center of levity" instead of a "center of gravity".

It is entirely up to you. . . You may choose to experience the old fantasies about the world and the spirit, or you may somehow with great effort and incredible conscious suffering far beyond the endurance of any ordinary human being, try to piece together a new universe—new of course, only for your psyche, but quite familiar to your essence—but to do this with any degree of integrity and to do this gently and not in the midst of terror requires a knowledge of the application of Real Science and Objective Art.

It is just this kind of manufacture of —or remanufacture of—a universe which creates the situation in which you must learn—and quickly—how to create action and thought. Incidentally, it requires the mastery of a subject entirely unknown to humans as a general thing—the subject of the basic structure of universes.

In order to appreciate the situation, you should approach all this from the viewpoint of a disinterested party. If you viewed this universe from outside, all you would be able to see would be the gross formations of space—you would be unable to see or sense the passage of time, movement, or the experience of being an object in space and time. In this state, a subjective analysis of the universe is impossible. And so you would in all likelihood decide to enter the universe as a particle of matter, in order to see what it is like. Imagine what your feelings would be, if once inside, you discovered that you were stuck in there for the duration of that universe, and that only after the universe completely dissipated would you be released from it.

You might decide to wait it out as a single particle, or as a series of rocks. Or you might decide to ride through the evolutionary cycles of a million or so planets. But you will be able to occupy objects and space in a universe only insofar as you are able to accept the sensations of form and consciousness.

So this Inner Room which exists apart from all other forms of reality is similar to the greater universe, except that it is only conceptualized mentally, and does not exist in solid form.

It is similar to the outer universe in that one can learn only those things which apply within that space, and that once outside that space, nothing learned there can be applied. It is also something that takes us further and further away from our intention to observe without drifting off into other subjects the incidents proceeding at Alex's Borscht Bowl—and we must find out now, before it is too late, what goes on there—or we might be led, perhaps never to return, into the fantastic worlds of Inner World entrances, Outer space beings, deserts, sod huts, magicians' houses, djinn, hotel rooms, and—if we aren't careful—God alone knows what. Next thing you know, we might go so far into daydreams that we find ourselves discussing the shape of God.

Which is interesting, because as it happens, one of the discussions which took place among the patrons at Alex's Borscht Bowl was on exactly that same subject.

"Say, what shape is God today?" one of them asked.

"Round," was the matter-of-fact reply. "Like a bottle whose spout turns into itself and comes out again without going through the sides."

"And what is God doing in a shape like that?" asked another.

"Pouring," came the response. "From the Empty into the Void."

They are all gone now, these inhabitants of Alex's Borscht Bowl. Alex sold the place, and then it went broke. They have all found new habitations uptown somewhere, and perhaps they meet now in a restaurant in which bright fluorescent lights glare down from the ceiling, and bus-boys clear chessboards with the rest of the dishes. But I am in quite another uptown restaurant that is soon to be closed also, here on the west side of central park.

And in this restaurant another brotherhood—formed only recently, but along ancient lines—will soon meet. But soon I will be gone, to California in order to as is said "seek other people's fortunes"—and also, if necessary, dig with my bare hands an entrance to the Inner World for those who come to work with me on these little ideas of mine.

CHAPTER NINE

THE REAL & COMPLETE ESOTERIC KNOWLEDGE

Now that which was hidden shall at last come to light—
and of course the only reason that it was hidden in this
late chapter was to keep it secret from those without patience, for whom it would be useless anyway. In order to
develop the power to use and apply this knowledge, one
must have at least a little humor and a real feeling for that
great maxim: "No sugar without a little tzimmus".

I have only allowed myself the pleasure of revealing this
little secret because it has been by now thoroughly guarded
by the Dogs of Boredom—the fierce enemy of the occultist
and "spiritual groupie", who have by now almost certainly
dropped far out of the picture.

It is safe then, to begin here to unravel this highly esoteric
mystery, now that all the so to say "spiritual riff-raff" have
in a manner of speaking "Met Their Maker".

Look around you. . . No doubt you see some sort of room.
Or perhaps you are reading this "outside" somewhere, and
you see around you a field, stream and trees. Very well, consider that to be a room. It is all the same room. Or at any
rate it is all the same to me where you read this. In fact, I
don't care whether or not you read this book at all. But on
the other hand, if you decide not to buy and read this book,
how will it be possible for me to collect the royalties so necessary to support this little habit of mine . . . *to introduce
into the life of ordinary humans the data necessary to attain
conscious life, and so forth and so on . . . .?*

You must by now also have realized in your common presence—or at least in one of your centers of thinking—that you could not possibly bring this book with you into the room in which it is most needed—the Inner World Room. It cannot be transported into the Inner World—but it is possible, with knowledge, to furnish the Inner World with knowledge from this book.

And so, according to Objective Knowledge which I discovered quite by chance, during certain experimental elucidations of mine carried out in inaccessible communities among certain members of secret brotherhoods not even known to ordinary humans, *you can take it with you.*

Of course, given the chance to fully realize what you are presently made up of, you may not want to. Be that as it may, the opportunity is there for you. It might be better to deal in an entirely new way with each new experience. That means—don't memorize these instructions.

The problem for me, as I begin to see now really clearly for the first time, is how to determine without doubt that you are ready to receive this knowledge—not in the manner normal to contemporary humans—that is, "by the process of automatic osmosis".

Now, I know—and you also are no doubt aware—that there is really no Great Secret Of The Universe other than the secret that *there is no secret.*

We all know that this self-same repetitive secret unfolds to everyone not only a little at a time, but again and again and again.

All right. I am now prepared, as you can easily see, to impart to you, without even looking first with my Inner Eye, to see if you can take it, this Great And Terrible Secret. That is to say, I have made with myself the conscious and of course intentional decision to unfold completely and without hesitation the entire secret, without too much concern for the delicate psyche, although if you do "freak out" as a result, I will feel a certain amount of sympathy. Well, there is no putting it off. Prepare now to hear the Greatest Secret ever imparted to man!

CHAPTER TEN

THE REALLY REAL GREAT & TERRIBLE SECRET!

Without fooling around, I feel that I should in all fairness warn you once again that this Great and Terrible Secret is soon coming up. You have no doubt since the reading of the previous chapter, put the book down for a few days of serious reflection—pondering whether to go through with this or not—a decision for which you, and you alone, can be held responsible.

Or perhaps you have been reading this straight through, in which case I suggest that you give your eyes a rest. It is absolutely amazing how some people—I among them—drive the organism far beyond its ordinary capacity. We seem to act as if the psyche and the body have the same unlimited energy as the essence has, and ask them to continue to function long after they require replenishment of the life force upon which they depend so completely.

That is to say, we do not properly pace ourselves according to the limits of the body and psyche. It is as if time compressed and expanded at irregular intervals all of which occurred at completely random periods, and which were triggered by the function of the organism, psyche, and actions of the habits contained in the essence, all acting quite independently of each other.

But don't concern yourself with that little problem. That wasn't the Great and Terrible Secret I had in mind.

I might as well begin, as it is becoming more and more apparent that this stalling is not going to make things any easier either for you or for me regarding the transmission of this secret.

We know that nothing will come of knowledge unless it can be applied—that ninety percent of knowledge is the ability to use it in a practical way. Even if one learns to use this secret, however, it does not guarantee that anything of value will be transmitted along with it, or that this little secret, which I am about to impart to you very soon. . .yes, very soon now, will do you any good at all.

But this should not concern you now. After all, you are busy developing your spiritual side, and so if you remain true to your aim to ignore all ordinary ideas and the cares of everyday life, you should do as well as anybody.

Can it be? I have just now constated that the sensations and feelings proceeding within my organism and also some other sensations and feelings proceeding within me but *not* within the organism, may have been somehow evoked in me in a way not immediately perceived by my awareness.

That is to say, I have just now noticed once again, even though on the first few instances I did not mention it, not believing it to be of any importance or interest, but now realizing that it does have some importance or it would not have occurred again and again during this narrative— that for the sixth time in less than five minutes of subjective time, my fingers—tips first, of course—are disappearing into the keyboard of this typewriter.

And I have definitely recognized now its real importance to you, the reader, because this peculiar sensation and perception was not precipitated in me in the usual way—that is, by my own conscious intention to relate to the universe— but rather, is proceeding in me in a quite automatic way. Realizing this, I can now state without doubt that in some way it was a direct result aroused in myself as a result of writing this material now being manifested for your benefit.

That is, the written material must in some way have stimulated in my organism this condition of semi-solidity.

This could very well be the case, because I have often noted in others and also in myself, a certain dissolution of the material form whenever this secret is imparted, or whenever it is about to be imparted, even casually or by accident.

So. . .just to be on the safe side, make certain that you have your material form all in order, balanced and in harmony, and anchored somehow in whatever degree necessary so that this Great and Terrible Secret will not, by its disclosure, completely dissolve and dissipate off into outer space the organic form currently inhabited by you and required by your psyche for the remainder of its transitory existence—and remain in this calm and centered state throughout the rest of this little discourse.

You have probably noticed by now that, in spite of the total disappearance of my fingers, the type has been appearing in accordance with my intentional wishes upon the paper. If this is an illusion, which is the illusion? That the type is getting onto the paper, or that my fingers have disappeared, or that I am the one who is causing the type to appear in the first place, or that you are able to perceive type on paper which originated from an imaginary source that you have chosen to call "Mr. Gold"?

I mention this only to let you know definitely that no feelings of guilt should exist regarding that little quirk of yours—that of talking with a mouth, listening with ears, thinking with the brain, acting with the body, eating with the stomach, breathing with the lungs, walking with the feet and legs, and beating time with the rythm of the heart.

You do not even have to apologize for racing blood through the organism just to supply "oxygen" to the "cells". In fact, you do not even need to apologize for your tendency to "die" and to be "reborn" in more or less frequent and predictable intervals. I realize that all this has become with you habitual, and far beyond your conscious control.

Now I must really get off the pot, as is said, and tell you what you wish to know. The problem is, what do you wish to know? There are, after all, so many things to know, and one cannot know all of them. Therefore it is obvious that a choice must be made between one form of knowledge and another. This question must—before I waste my time by telling you something that you do not wish to use in a practical way—in my opinion be fully settled before we begin.

But on the other hand, there is only one Great and Terrible Secret. And now suddenly as I recall the material contained on the previous several pages, I seem to sense and even to recognize directly in my essence among all the other knowledge contained in it, now that it has fully aroused my psyche for the creation of this autobiographical sketch I am writing for your edification and I hope for your real arousal of enthusiasm toward these ideas for yourself, a certain something, which—if I did not know better—would indicate to me that in some way or other, I have "slipped it to you" already. That is to say, I have inadvertently presented to you, before I was ready to, this Great and Terrible Secret.

Yes, I see that this is true. It has already been presented in the previous material in at least fourteen different forms. Well, then, there is no sense in going on further about this, is there?

But on the other hand. . . even though I have already stated this secret several times, I should perhaps put it into simple everyday words, so that even a dense receiver such as the human psyche can understand it, in accordance with that peculiarity of the human mind which prevents the assimilation of any data it does not like or does not agree with—of course measured against only already existing beliefs—even when the appropriate shock has been administered with it.

I could of course concur with the Ancient Brotherhoods in the method of transmission of secrets by first giving a little introduction to it for the next twenty years just to see if you are genuinely sincere—and willing to learn to apply and master it.

Or I could couch the secret within a parable—an analogy—
in which the secret has been hidden, and from which you
could decipher the secret once in possession of the Key.

Or I could put the secret into all capital letters—or perhaps in italics. But after only one or two words written in
all caps or italics you would become, as is quite common
among humans of the contemporary issue, tired of reading
something written in only one typeface—as you no doubt
are already equally bored with this typeface—and your attention would tend to wander away into realms more profitable for your imagination.

And besides all that, you might not even recognize the
importance of a passage written entirely in capital letters
or italics, in which case you might simply read it with the
"Ninety Percent Comprehension According To the Evelyn
Wood Reading Dynamics Method Of Superficial Assimilation Of Data" to the point of scanning just like a robot until it was all safely tucked away in the automatic Verbatim
Repeating Portion of the psyche.

But what is that you say? You have used this wonderful
new reading method and can now repeat verbatim every
word you have ever read since you began using it? Then
perhaps you would like to give a monotone recital of this
work of mine also.

Still another method of assuring complete transmission
of this secret not only into your psyche, but also into your
essence, d-i-r-e-c-t through your belly button, so to speak,
is to give you many chances to prepare your attention for
reception of the secret.

By giving you so many opportunities to focus your awareness on this question, you should be able eventually to bring
your attention to bear on it without having to chase around
after it as if you were a dog-catcher trying to collar a mad
dog with your bare hands. That is to say, I have more or
less given you a net with which to catch the dog and teach
it to sit still for a moment or two.

But just at this moment another thought has struck my now quite active mentation. That is, my own dog catcher has just now caught a stray dog. And this dog—or thought, to you—is: *If it were important enough to you, you would pay attention even if an army of murderous cannibals were on your tail.*

So now, finally, I have come to realize that my task is to somehow arouse in your already very charming and apathetic state sufficient interest in these ideas that they become for you—at least on a temporary basis—important enough so that you will pay attention. That means that I must in some way raise your level of awareness and interest to the degree of reason called *aviuncharajijigronamol,* or Interested More Than Mildly.

And so, it will first be necessary for me to demonstrate to you the nature of the secret and so eventually to arouse in you as a result, some idea of its importance to you.

But what could I say about its nature that hasn't already been said a thousand. . . no, a million or more. . . times? Why is it so important to learn this secret? What good will it do you to know this secret? Is it the same secret that the ancients possessed? Is there an afterlife? Does telepathy really work? Does man have a soul? Is there a doctor in the house? How's tricks? What's new?

Perhaps the answer to these truly important questions is to simply lie back in your easy chair and watch television.

It has just now occurred to me—suddenly, as usual—that it might be difficult to try to transmit this by communication—psyche to psyche. Perhaps it needs to be transmitted directly from being to being. On the other hand, maybe it is difficult because I don't know what I'm talking about. Oops. In that case it would require so much apology for my wiseacring that it would be incomparably inconvenient for both of us.

And so, we might as well get on with it. You will find it in the next chapter, if everything goes well. . . And why now should it all of a sudden go well?

CHAPTER ELEVEN

THE SAGA OF HUNCHEL IRAGAN

Before I begin this narrative, I feel that I should explain
at least a little of its origin and how I came to acquire it.
Only after a long search among the inaccessible communities in hidden areas of the world did I come into contact
with a certain Brotherhood...*the existence of which was
not even recorded among the surviving Ancient Brotherhoods.*

After making initial contact with this community, I remained with them for two years before anything was open
to me.

I managed to make friends with one of the brothers, although with difficulty, due to the strictly enforced vow of
silence.

Brother Geghs began to look after me as if I were his
fraternal younger brother, and so it was that in time I was
invited to hear in a meeting reserved only for long-time res-
idents who had taken full vows—I had not taken even partial vows—the central hymn or "Heroic Saga" about the
founder of their Brotherhood, the man who was known as
Father Hunchel Iragan.

This song regarding the founder had passed down through
oral tradition for over ten thousand years, and remains un-
changed to the present day, as I was later to determine when
I found references to certain passages of text which had been
unearthed during the International Geophysical Year, which
showed beyond a doubt the absolutely unaltered state of
their oral tradition which had begun thousands of years ago.

I was fortunate enough to bring with me my "steel-trap mind" which recorded as well as any tape recorder every word of the portion of the saga which I was privileged to hear.

I should also mention that when the Chief Abbot learned of this mistake regarding my presence during the singing of this Heroic Saga of theirs, he ordered my immediate dismissal from the community.

But I had gotten what I came there for, and had paid for it with two years of work for the community—and hard work, too. No, I had not been idle during those two years, and perhaps the Abbot recognized this and it was his way to present this material in this fashion.

I knew very well—and indeed, had told the Father Abbot this upon entering the community—that I had no calling to become a "preserver", although I realized the value of that profession, but rather to become an "applier" of knowledge. And in this way I believe he granted this wish of mine, both consciously and intentionally, as stated to him at the beginning of our acquaintence.

And so, without further hesitation, I will make a translation as well as is possible into english—granting that in my native language, there are certain essence and idea words notably missing, thanks to the contemporary disinterest in such ideas.

THE SAGA OF HUNCHEL IRAGAN

The saga of Hunchel Iragan is at a beginning,
Dabanag who forms the evening and the morning,
Lifting up the birds of sunrise,
Flames in glory of the sun.

Rising upward in the terror of the womb,
Into the darkness of the Heart of Mar,
Into the coaldust eyes peeping from the face,
Of Hayr the White-Faced One.

Now he flies into the light,
The Indanik of thrumming heart,
Treading now the hidden darkness,
Coming now into the Land of Light.

He was alone and stood his ground,
He was and knew his name,
The name that was not uttered by himself,
But by the mankind scattered in the brilliant stars.

And in that timeless space where stars
Remained like crystal ornaments suspended,
He was, and serpent coils unwound around him,
Like a creature shrouded, waiting for the light.

The shadow, too, was gone with waking brow,
The way was lost forever,
Gardens of Delight were melted,
Like the molten lava into flowing light.

And inside out, yet rightside in,
He felt ecstatic union, all things known,
And thing flowed into thing until all things were one,
Until the lonely eye turned inward to itself and knew
                                        its name.

And slowly dawned the Will of Whimless Knowledge,
Firm it was, and as the nature of the light,
That all must be undone that ever was,
Returning to the Land Where Shadow Never Lies.

Alone, alone, alone, thought he, that was alone no more,
For speaking thoughts the speaker must be known,
And only then he knew his name,
His name was Hunchel Iragan.

His name which he alone could utter,
Never said but once by anyone aloud,
In every million million years of time,
And now the yearless year, within the Land of Light.

Remorseful then, he made a star appear,
And move, and change its course,
And yet, no matter what he did,
All time, all space, would pass into He Knew.

Endless, Still, the rumbling of the night
Patterned with the tracings of his endless thought,
Trembled with the weight of mighty knowledge,
Passing in the end into the Light of Truth.

The water of his sweat dripped down the brow,
Which saw all things and knew all truth,
He saw this not, and wove the pattern deeper,
Yet even then he Knew the Truth.

His eyes ablaze, kindled with the flame of raging might,
Lips drawn back in battle,
Mercy in her fiery grief had whetted them with pity,
He calmed himself submitting to the victor.

Now warfare's at an end for him,
And he may fashion at his leisure,
Splendid coils woven into carpets fine,
Interspun like webbing made by mother spider.

Silken surfaces like water,
Lapping at the rock upon which
Father serpent sits,
Spinning Lies and Telling Tales.

A cry has echoed through the Land of Light,
And so another dream has passed,
Across the brow of Father All-Things,
Uttered in the stillness of the child's laughter.

Someday the time will come when shadows lie once more,
When creeping darkness will obliterate the Truth,
When all will sense and know and understand and feel,
When one is essence, only then can life be real.

    I have only included this astonishing song, preserved by the Brotherhood I mentioned, because it was, in my opinion, an important and accurate—yet succinct—exposition of the Great and Terrible Secret, and moreover, since another individual wrote it, and not myself, it will be much more likely to strike a real impression in the reader.

    I have been now for the past several chapters engaged in writing material which, according to all factors personally elucidated by me regarding the format of such books as this, is required of the author in order to assure the reader—and any interested large paperback publisher—that this book is indeed of the expected status.

That is to say, I have now, in my opinion, produced sufficient wordage to convince anyone that this book correctly matches the public idea of books falling into the category "spiritual".

Now that I have more than fulfilled this requirement of contemporary man in regard to "this type" of book, I would like to write along lines more in keeping with my real feelings, and also not just coincidentally more in keeping with my aim for you regarding your essence— regardless of your own aim for your essence which I am more than sure somehow involves the use of a garbage compactor at least insofar as the perpetuation of the fantasy regarding your psyche and its reality is concern- ed. That is to say, I am sure that your psyche is deter- mined to survive at any cost. . . And I am equally deter- mined to help you dissolve it somehow, leaving the simple—and to some, very dull—essence in its place on a more or less permanent basis.

And so, I am grimly insistent on writing a little some- thing about childrens' games, which you will find in the next chapter. . . Or you can just toss this book away in disgust and forget the whole thing. It really wasn't ex- actly what you expected, was it?

CHAPTER TWELVE

THE CAROUSEL STORY

As I recall it now, there was always a central theme to all the games we played when young. Perhaps you remember this "central theme" of all games played by all children of the human race everywhere on the planet earth. This central theme could be stated simply as: *To Always And In Everything, Be The Last Kid On The Block*. All games, regardless of their harmless outer form, were played with this same basic survival aim.

And this common aim of ours, expressed of course only inwardly and regarding only oneself, was the chief cause of the dangerous risks we took even in the most mild and harmless play.

I recall with especial vividness one particular incident in which I was forced—by my own bravado—to walk along the ledge of the ninth floor of the Hotel Ansonia on Broadway, during an extremely windy day, as a result of a game of "follow the leader", which up until then had been a quite sane occupation.

The hotel was primarily occupied by artists, musicians, and theater people—among whom were my friend Danny and his mother. On this day, Danny, another friend, Manuel, and I sat on the ledge after having completed the dare.

As we sat on the ledge, with our legs dangling over the side, the window opened very slowly, but almost startling us with a psychic force nearly sufficient to convince us to involuntarily drop to the cement pavement below.

The ledge was not very wide, but neither were we. Since we were reasonably small compared to the width of the ledge, we could hold our balance in spite of the strong wind. Only Danny came anywhere close to his "inevitable candidacy for the next world" when his mother opened the window, but Manual and I grabbed him just in time. My attention was on his mother, who had remained at least outwardly quite calm during all this. We had learned long ago that there was no point trying to scare her, as we were able to do with other adults.

She was an opera singer, and occasionally went on tour for several months, during which time Danny stayed with us. She was by now used to our expressions of being which often took the form of awful—unless viewed from above—risks to our material bodies, and had resolved not to make too much of a fuss over it, or to respond with hysteria.

"That's very dangerous, boys," she said.

"Yes, we know, mother," Danny replied. "Would you rather we did something else?"

"No," she said. "I have a feeling it would be something even worse."

"Then it's okay if we stay out here?"

"If you wish. But you might want to come inside now, anyway. We have a very unusual visitor, who has offered to make a special kind of dinner for all of us, and to play some unusual music afterward."

"Who is he?" I asked.

"Will he tell us a story?" Danny asked—he was always hungry for stories because he wanted to be a comedian.

"Maybe, but you yourselves will have to ask him," she said particularly firmly.

We went in through the window as usual, and ran inside to wash. As we competed for the soap and water, we could smell the aroma of cooking coming from the small convenience kitchen. The odors were strange even to us, who had become used to everything from Russian food to Puerto-Rican food.

But this . . . Was somehow different. It had a delicious aroma, like some kind of edible incense.

Out of the kitchen came a short man—but tall to us then, of course—wearing a dark blue suit now pretty well worn, so that it had a shine to it. His head was almost completely bald, except for the short fuzz of white hair around the ears and back of the head. He had a big curled white moustache, and his face was mottled with liver spots and wrinkles formed around the sides of his eyes, but hardly any on the forehead. He was fairly heavy-set, and looked as if he had at one time or another wrestled or lifted weights. His face had the character of someone who has suffered a lot, and yet who has never allowed worries to touch him inside.

He smiled and I felt instantly that I was in the presence of Santa Claus. This uncanny sensation of inner warmth was so unusual for me that I resolved instantly to someday discover the means of imparting to others that same feeling on first meeting them. And later, when I attained all those powers as a result of my searches, even they were nothing compared to my genuine wish for this single attribute above all others.

"It is custom of mine," he said, "to make little something from each country every evening, especially when among Americans." And so we ate this marvellous food, in silence as usual, sitting on the floor among all the memorabilia of opera, white silk upholstered furniture, white wall to wall carpeting—unusual for that time—and the giant concert grand piano.

After the meal, he pulled some candy out of his overcoat pocket, and as we ate it he played on a small Indian organ, operated by pumping with one hand and playing with the other.

"Soon I must go to my own rooms. I have some very important people coming to see me tonight and I must prepare for them something *Khotseli*—something to wake them up and make them take notice. But for now—is there anything you would like to do? I prefer to be here with you than with adults, but I have only limited time to indulge myself for my own being."

"Do you know any stories?" Danny instantly asked. We all sensed that this man was a story-teller, with that wonderful instinct proper to the beings of young persons of high interest in ordinary and exotic life.

Unfortunately we never did learn the name of this mysterious visitor, and afterward he left, accompanied by Danny's mother, who seemed to know him quite well— perhaps from Russia, before she left for the United States.

This is the story told to us by our unusual visitor:

"I may say some things during the course of this story upsetting to young boys, but there is a reason for everything I say. If I tell too much, you must then stop me, and I will instead tell you another story."

Once, many years ago in this subjective flow we call time, there lived a carousel. I say "lived" and I mean exactly that, but you must not think that I mean that this carousel—an ordinary wooden "merry-go-round" decorated on its surface with brass ornaments, paintings and gilded mirrors, breathed, ate, slept and conversed the same as you and I.

No, not exactly the same. Why, you would have to have looked very closely to even notice its slow breathing. And you might never have noticed—unless you were making very close observation—the way in which it studied each little boy and girl who came aboard for a ride.

It had a very thoughtful appearance at that time, and one might easily wonder what it had up its sleeve.

For many years now, this carousel lacked nothing for its ordinary needs. It had always enough of every type of food necessary to a carousel, and it had treats on the week-ends. You see, this carousel was exactly the same as all other carousel in regard to its nutritional requirements: that is to say, it ate little children.

As the horses spun faster and faster, and the dazzling lights flashed in the eyes of the mothers and nannies, and sounds of bright music momentarily soothed and calmed the appointed guardians of the children, the squat little wurlitzer organ would emerge from the darkest shadows in the center of the carousel, and snatch one of the children to carry him or her off into the depths of the interior of the carousel.

This action of the carousel would go completely undetected by the parents or nannies. They always believed that the child had gotten off the carousel on its other side. But they never thought the child might have been eaten by the carousel, because of its inanimate—at least to them—nature. No one ever suspects a carousel.

But in one respect this carousel was different from all other carousels. It considered itself to be a very moral carousel. Of course, most other carousels considered themselves to be moral, too, but not as moral as this one. It would not eat just any child who wandered on. . . No, no, no! The only children that it would consider eating were those who remained on the carousel for more than three rides. In short, it would eat only greedy children.

But after many years at the "same old stand", things began to go not quite so well for this very moral carousel. Certain things were beginning to happen which were beyond its control and which had a very negative effect on this carousel's ability to remain true to its aim of maintaining its morality.

The paint, once brand new and shiny, now began to peel and to crack. The wood began in places to rot away, and nobody responsible for its upkeep seemed to notice for a very long time. It was not, in fact, until it became commercially inconceivable to repair it that anyone took notice at all of its condition.

The expensive and almost impossible to replace mirrors with their gilded frames were no longer manufactured by anyone since their original maker had closed shop in favor of factories which began to mass-produce "modern marvellous designs". They had become cracked and some had fallen off, while others had been deliberately removed by vandals. The painted scenes of sylphs and fauns were faded and encapsulated with dirt beyond repair.

Almost everything on the carousel required repair work of some kind, or complete replacement, both of which were impossible at that time. There was no one left who could do such repair work. They had all gone into other trades, as they no longer were in demand at their skills. People had gotten into a habit of simply buying a new item when the old one failed to work.

Fewer children came to ride, because this carousel was in such bad condition. Less and less money became available for its upkeep, until it was completely impossible to even hope that something could be done.

Only one or two children came to ride each day, and because it was not much fun for them to ride an old battered horse with a missing tail and no reins, they did not stay on for long. Some—only a few—remained for two rides, but never for three.

It was now impossible for the carousel to obtain even for its most urgent needs just a few greedy children. In fact, it had not eaten anything at all now for over one full year. It would of course not even consider eating a child who remained for only one or two rides.

And so, after a while of this, it came to a very important decision. It decided to take active part in this problem, even if it had to create an entirely new solution. It had up to that time depended upon its owner to do something, but it was becoming more and more obvious that the owner did not intend to take any action to help it.

It was time now for the carousel to emerge from its passive role and play a more aggressive one.

As far as the carousel could see, it had only two choices, since it did not have within its private means enough capital to arrange for its own repairs.

The first alternative was to leave for greener pastures, to either find food, or money for repairs. The second idea was to lower the moral standards by one ride. That is, to eat only those children who remained for two rides. But it also recognized that things were not getting any better, and that eventually the standards would have to be lowered to one ride, and then maybe it would end up having to chase children all over the park. In short, it would become an ordinary carousel in all respects, and lose every shred of its decency and morality. It would be no better than all of those immoral carousels. And so it decided on the first choice, to leave and seek its fortune.

This unhappy and very, very hungry carousel, after firmly making this decision to leave, picked up its flat running skirt and brass ring holder, and clumped away through the park as quietly as is possible for a carousel more than fifty feet in diameter and weighing in excess of ten thousand kilograms.

It traveled by night, and by day it squatted on its haunches hoping that someone would come for a ride. But nobody came to ride on the carousel, because it was old and no longer pretty, and because it was in the wild—that is to say, it was in the woods, and not in its proper place in a nice park with a well-trimmed lawn.

And so, further and further afield it was led by hunger and also incidentally by its mental suffering. Yes, it suffered very much. It did not consciously realize it, but it missed the gay laughter and excitement of the little children.

And so, all night long during this carousel's quest for suitable food, the quiet and stillness of the evening was broken by the muffled sobs and falling tears—of not inconsiderable size—coming from this very unhappy carousel.

And each night the carousel stopped—just before dawn—in order to rest. And as it did so, the wood-folk were stirred a moment by the emanations of suffering coming from the carousel, and then assured that they were not personally in danger, they stretched, scratched, and turned over to sleep again even more soundly than before, thanks to the soothing effect of their unwilling and miserable guardian.

Each morning the carousel hoped that it would be somehow different. Every day it waited, in the hope that in some way something would change by itself. Then finally one hopeless day its heart broke with self-pity, and all hope perished. The helpless carousel sat on the ground not even trying any more to look beautiful, and it cried from the very depths of its hunger. It cried, and cried and cried. It was not until the feelings of frustration and desperation had subsided a little that the carousel realized that nothing real had been accomplished either by its journey or by its suffering.

Suddenly it came to the understanding that it had been hoping that as a result of its deep suffering and anguish, someone or other would appear and take pity on it—that some benefactor would come out of the woods and because it was so miserable, the benefactor would fix everything—give it new life.

"Ah, what a fantasy I have been having!" exclaimed the carousel with a new found feeling of freedom. "Now I realize how foolish it is to hope for a benefactor who will come to my rescue just because of my suffering. Everyone else suffers, too, in their own inner world, and because of that no one else can see my suffering no matter how strongly I manifest it to others. And even if they did become aware of it, no one would come to my aid simply because I am suffering. No—I must give them some gratification in return, unless they are a complete altruist.

Moreover, I must if I hope to find a benefactor, make all possible persons aware of this intention of mine to offer gratification in return corresponding to the amount of effort and help given to me by them. Now that I fully recognize this, I must also begin to see the problem as it really is."

So saying, the carousel suddenly knew that it had been trying to solve its problem in the wrong way. It had before this only realized that it was hungry. Now, finally, it came to the realization of what it had been hungry *for*. Up to now it had been simply "chasing its own hunger", rather than finding something which would satisfy the hunger. And since the only thing that would satsify its hunger was greedy children, and they would not come to him as he was, he had to seek out a sufficient quantity of greedy children who were visible as greedy children without having to take the test of remaining for three rides.

Now all the very moral carousel had to do was to find some greedy children, discover how to tell them apart from other children, and how to attract them or catch them in their native habitat. And so it was in this way that the very moral carousel decided to embark immediately for the country of America.

On the boat to the American Continent, the carousel acquired the habit of standing at the railing of the ship, and while looking out over the waves, to ponder its possible fate there in America.

While there was no doubt the largest possible concentration of greedy children in America, according to reliable reports of other carousels who had been there previously—there was still the problem of catching or attracting them.

The carousel was not entirely foolish, and now that it had its reason back after its little episode of self-pity and suffering, it could ponder even the most serious question without too much trouble. It realized that if it tried any direct action toward the children of America, it could be deported. Even here on the boat it was not precisely as anonymous as it would have liked to be, in spite of traveling "incognito" and wearing dark glasses.

And it also recognized that catching greedy children by any direct means—such as running after them—was not acceptable, because it left no means for the correct determination of the presence of greed, if any was there. You must remember that this was a very essential factor to this very moral carousel. Without long and careful observation it would be impossible to determine the character of the children, unless they came to ride. It realized the foolhardiness of trying to follow the children all about town observing them for indications of greed.

The carousel realized that it must find some other way other than its former youthful attraction to draw the youngsters close to it, and moreover find some way to make it worthwhile for them to remain for three rides.

But along with this arousal of thought, came the inevitable results of intentional thought. The carousel suddenly was able to constate within itself the concept of efficiency. "Why attract everyone?" it reasoned. "If it is possible to only attract the greedy, I will have a much better choice, and besides that, I will have to make less effort as well."

And before the ship landed on the American shore, the carousel learned from a steam-organ fellow passenger who was also going to the American Continent for much the same reason, something it could not possibly have discovered about Americans unless it had been there or come in contact with another carousel who had been there before.

This fact was simply that the Americans had instilled in themselves an unconscious hatred for the articles currently manufactured by mass production, and that this instinctive hatred manifested itself in a love for the old—especially the exotic old.

"Then you think they will like me?" the carousel asked the steam organ.

"Oh, yes, and particularly you. Why, you look over a century old!" it exclaimed.

"Is that important?" the carousel asked.

"Important? Why, if you are over one hundred years old, no matter *what* you are, and regardless of your condition, you will be an instant celebrity!"

The carousel, who was not only very moral, but also equally cunning, immediately made up a sign which he placed on one of the horses. The card read: "Genuine Antique. . . Over 100 Years Old."

Naturally, when he got off the boat, and even before he stepped completely off the landing plank, he was a great success with the Americans. Soon he was installed in his very own place in the "Great Central Park Area", and suddenly all kinds of food became available to him. He was so certain of his success that he even told some reporters from newspapers who had come to interview him that he had the habit of eating greedy little children.

And instead of reacting with horror to this little indiscretion of his, the reporters laughed and said among themselves how "cute" he was. After a while, everyone got so used to the joke of a carousel eating little children, thanks to the repetition of this joke automatically and incessantly by the other newspapers, he was actually able to walk into a restaurant across the street from the park and order his specialty.

And in his honor and because he was such a celebrity, they even named that restaurant after his "special plate"— and today that same restaurant still stands. In fact, the Child's Restaurant is now one of the great tourist attractions of that city, thanks to the patronage of the very moral carousel.

But then catastrophe struck! With all the sudden fame came vast amounts of money—and before the carousel was able to make its escape, it had a "business agent" and a "manager", and in short order workmen had arrived with fresh paint and new mirrors made especially at a very high cost to be just like the originals, and brass fittings, polish, and glue. The painted scenes were restored by experts to their original bright hues, and the faded dullness of the old carousel was brought to its first-class original intensity only dimly remembered in the far-distant—but not *that* distant— past.

The organ was re-tuned, and the bells, chimes and drums were all repaired. The horses were glued and repaired, their tails and reins replaced, and soon the carousel looked in all respects just like a brand new carousel. The worst thing in an antique market had occurred to it. The carousel had been *restored*.

It considered leaving forever the shelter of its new protective barn, which had been constructed around it to protect it from the weather, as with all this restoration it had become quite valuable.

It thought of walking in the damp evening weather in order to perhaps lose some of its newly acquired beauty. It hoped to become mildewed enough to once again "pass for an antique". It was even prepared to lie about its age.

But it was not necessary for the carousel to partially destroy itself in order to eat. For one thing, it had a "charge account" at the restaurant, and for another as it sat pondering the new situation, a new thought occurred to it.

With the steady downpour of cold rain falling outside, the carousel sat pondering this new thought. It was warm and dry inside this shelter in spite of the rain, and for once in its existence it had a real home. It wished to remain until the end of its days in the snug warmth of this shelter. It liked the smell of damp wood that was not its own wooden form getting wet, and it enjoyed the sound of the rainfall drumming steadily on the roof in its slow tapping rhythm.

It liked to be dry when everything else was wet outside, and to hear and smell the rain, and to see between the cracks in the barn sides the wetness outside without having to be itself drenched in the rain. It would have to find another new solution to the problem, something besides ruining itself or running away.

And as always in such a crisis, realization had come. Who besides greedy children would be willing and able to pay the new price—the same as for a "Broadway Show"—for a simple ride on a carousel?

The carousel also knew that, thanks to the curious psyches of the people of the American Continent, it did not have to determine who was greedy and who was not. Here, *everyone* was greedy! And so, when the new owner came by to open up, the very moral carousel ate him, and went into business for himself."

So finishing his story, the old Russian immigrant slowly rose, and taking leave of us said:

"You, and not the older ones, are my hope for the future. They are already too crystallized to even begin work. I wish for you to remember *every word and every detail of this story*. This is most important for you and for me. Goodbye."

And he left with Danny's mother for his "important meeting" downstairs. I never saw him again after that, until one day in Vancouver, British Columbia—but that is another story.

A few days later, I was playing a game of solo ringaleevio, the object of which, as I understand it, is to have the worst outfielder be "it", and the other players get lost so thoroughly that he gives up and goes home, so the rest of them can play baseball without having to choose him for either side.

One day, while I was elected to be "it"—as there was no doubt about my ability as an outfielder—I decided on that occasion to count to one thousand by tens, rather than to ten by ones. I enjoyed this so much that when I got to one hundred, I started counting by ones, and even occasionally by fractions.

And as I made this slow count there came into my automatically arising thought—now freed from other duties to the environment thanks to my occupation with counting—a strange mental sensation, and then an accompanying physical sensation.

This new sensation began first as a feeling similar to extreme boredom aroused by the inevitability of the situation. . . and then another quite different feeling began to be aroused—one of cheerful disinterest. Finally, this changed to a feeling as if I had left the body and had begun to fly through the air—although there was no sensation of movement, just perception of it.

Suddenly I found myself in a strange land—familiar to me normally only during periods of study at the school in which I, along with the other children, had been forced to learn to repeat verbatim certain data which I knew to be patently false regarding the imaginary history, science, mathematics, religions, and generally whitewashed barbarism of the human race, both ancient and modern.

When my traveling consciousness had come to a stop I found myself in some way able to stand upon a soft substance resembling cotton or sponge and which was colored a deep shade of orchid. Above and to the right at an apparently large distance stood a large castle of pseudo-teutonic design which had been erected atop a mound of the same substance that lay underfoot.

When I approached the castle, I did not have as far to walk as at first I had supposed—it was not nearly as far away or as large as it had seemed from my original position.

When the landscape is unbroken by other objects of known size which can be used for reference, it is impossible to determine the size or distance of one single object, unless it is an object of known size or known distance, in which case the corresponding factor can be determined.

In short, the castle was no larger than eight feet tall. Coming to the entrance, I was forced to crawl through the portcullis on my stomach. With my feet in the moat and my head in the Great Hall I stopped to listen and to look.

You may think that I am about to tell the story of Alice in Wonderland—and I must admit that I was sorely tempted. But I realize that with the high intelligence and keen faculties of observation among the well-educated readers of today, it would be immediately recognized as the story already told by Mr. Dodgson, and everyone would say "Why, that stupid so and so, he's telling the tale of Alice in Wonderland. We can't let him get away with that!"

I know that even the simplest child and the most complex adult knows the story of Alice well enough to spot the fraud. So I have decided instead to offer you a fraud that I know I can get away with. . .

When I could see around me inside that castle, I spotted the usual pile of junk you find around a giant's domicile. There were singing harps, geese laying golden eggs, assorted peasants and cattle being preserved by smoking and then being packaged in saran wrap. The critters were of course the corresponding diminutive size appropriate to an eight foot high castle. That meant the giant would be about two feet high, and sure enough, he was.

"Hi," the giant said, welcoming me with a grin.

"Hi, yourself," I replied.

As the giant and I muched on peanut butter and jelly sandwiches with hors d'ouvre of smoked villager on soda crackers, we settled back into a kind of comeraderie, and the giant decided to tell a story—which, as you know by now, I am almost always in the market for.

He stood with his hands behind his back and began a narrative in "nineteenth century schoolboy rehearsal style". That is, he talked as if he were a record player that had just been programmed to play back a recording he had never properly assimilated or understood.

CHAPTER THIRTEEN

YASSUN DEDE AND THE HOLY OF HOLIES

Somewhere along the shore of the *Sea of Sher,* where the sky falls dreamily blue upon the deep water, and the wind rolls softly across the cool sweet grassy slopes, and where, in short, everything is beautiful, there lived a tall and gaunt black-haired and dark-eyed young man by the name of Yassun Dede, who was, according to his mirror, just too beautiful a person to be a hog farmer.

But that is what he was, and so was his father, and his father's father, and so on as far back as anyone cared to remember. In short, he came from a family of hog farmers, and carried the tradition up to the present day.

But to escape his misery and disappointment he would wander far away in his imagination—far beyond the pig sty, beyond the little hut in which he lived alone since his parents had passed away.

His imagination took him into the land of ogres, castles, enchantments, and beautiful princesses—almost as beautiful as himself. But, alas for him, a hog farmer, due to certain results of his trade, has about as much chance for romance with a princess as a barf bag has to remain spotless during a thunderstorm over Kansas.

But fortunately for Yassun Dede, chance was with him. One day, while scattering the food in the trough, he was surprised to see a man of obvious nobility riding up to him. The man rode a great white stallion, and was dressed in velvet covered with a leather weskit. He carried a fin sword at his side, in a gold and silver tooled scabbard.

The stranger wheeled his horse up just short of where Yassun Dede stood frozen in amazement and wonder. The man leaned over to talk to Yassun.

"You are Yassun Dede? The hog-farmer Yassun Dede?"

Yassun Dede was at first very flattered that the nobleman had asked for him personally—but then he became suspicious, thinking that this might be a tax-collector or someone from the sheriff—maybe he had been accused of a crime or something. . . ?

"Why do you seek him, sir, if I may be so bold?"

"I have a task for him involving an enchanted castle, a magic sword, and the Holy of Holies," replied the nobleman.

"Well, then, you have come to the right place!" Yassun said, not able to contain his joy in the slightest. He had just known something like this would eventually happen to him.

"Well, then, my boy," the rider said, "you don't remember me, but then, you're not expected to. I happen to know that with your remarkable talents you will be able to perform this important task."

"What task is that, sir?"

"I want you to take this magic sword," he said, unbuckling it from his belt, "and go to the enchanted island of *Khojgor* in the Sea of *Girginum*, and there find the Holy of Holies, Most Precious of Precious, and bring it back to me. If you do this, you shall have your reward."

Yassun Dede could not believe his ears. At last his opportunity to leave hog-farming forever had come. Now he could return a hero, marry some well-to-do lady, and expect to give his descendents a better inheritance than a life of pig-farming.

"Oh, noble rider, you have made me the happiest man in the world," he said. "Now I can leave these stupid hogs forever! Yassun would have said much more, going into stunning detail, had not the nobleman already flung the sword down and ridden away before Yassun could get halfway cranked up on the subject.

In fact, had the noble rider remained, he would have heard nothing else from Yassun Dede but the miseries of hog-farming—which was the real reason he had not found a wife, but he did not realize the effect that his complaints had on young ladies with tender ears and even more tender thoughts.

All day long as Yassun Dede made his preparations to leave the hog farm and set off on his quest for adventure and glory, he hugged and kissed—of course only mentally— each hog wallowing in the pigsty, he was so overjoyed at the prospect.

"I'll never see another hog ever again," he sang. "I will get the Holy of Holies. . .With the magic sword it should be easy enough—and then I'll bring it back and collect my reward! Then I'll be married and have children and grandchildren. Perhaps I can get into a profession I can be really proud of! Won't it be wonderful! Goodbye, Priscilla! Goodbye, Esmeralda! Goodbye, Elmer! Goodbye, Susy!" And on and on he sang, all day, cheerfully ringing shouts of "Goodbye, goodbye!" to each of them, many times over.

Of course, being a practical man, he did not just turn the hogs loose to wander the countryside, but instead after saying goodbye to them and feeding them, he gave them to a neighbor of his to keep for him until he could return and sell them at the market.

The next morning, he left the now very quiet farm, and turning past the empty pigsty just as the sun rose over the hills, he walked off toward the promising horizon before him, in the direction indicated to him by the noble rider who had just given him his real task in life.

It was nearly one year later, and many interesting adventures since he had left his hated hog farm, when Yassun Dede finally came to the Sea of *Girginum*. He could see the Island of *Khojgor* and its enchanted castle lying not far offshore. But he could not swim there weighted down with the magic sword and scabbard, and he dared not leave it behind. Somehow he sensed that the danger of this adventure was just about to begin.

Looking about, he discovered soon that there was not a boat to be found anywhere. The ogres had destroyed them, lest anyone come unseen to the island.

Determined at all costs to reach the prize now so close, he began constructing a raft on which he could place the magic sword and scabbard, and which he could push to the island, swimming along behind it. That was an even better plan, he thought, than a boat. This way, he would be low in the water, and there would be less chance that he would be seen coming to the island.

And so he cut some timber and lashed it together. But as he bent to pick up an end of the lashing vine, a giant scorpion struck his left hand with its stinger.

Realizing that he had to act quickly, he cut the wound with the magic sword. But the power of the sword was so great that rather than the little cross-cut he had intended, the whole hand was chopped off as if it had been butter.

Fortunately, however, the wound healed instantly, thanks to the efficacy of the magic sword.

"Oh, well," he philosophized, "When I get back with the Holy of Holies and collect my reward, I can buy another hand—of silver. And I won't have to work at hard labor, so who needs it, anyway?"

And so he finished the raft, and placing the magic sword on top, he made his way to the water, dragging the raft along behind him.

But as he swam out toward the island, a huge sea monster came toward him. Seeing the monster before it could reach him, Yassun dragged himself halfway onto the raft, and taking the magic sword out of its finely crafted scabbard, he slashed around in the water until the monster, mortally wounded, swam off to die somewhere in the deep.

But after it was all over, Yassun discovered that he had in the heat of battle inadvertently chopped off his left foot.

"Never mind," he reasoned. "When I am rich, I can buy another one, of gold inlay and jewels. And I can be carried around on a litter by servants."

And so, reaching the shore of the island, he crawled up and made a crutch for himself out of a branch of wood.

When he got to the path leading to the castle, he was horrified to see a huge fire-breathing dragon standing directly in front of the entrance. Even though the dragon was quite large, Yassun had been so wrapped up in his thoughts regarding his triumphant return and subsequent wealth and importance that the dragon had been able to escape his attention until he was almost upon it.

Yassun brandished the magic sword. The dragon looked at the sword, and then at Yassun's wrist, noting the missing hand, and then at the leg, observing the absence of the left foot.

"Magic sword?" the dragon mildly inquired.

"You bet it is!" Yassun shouted, fearfully awaiting the dragon's attack.

"I rather thought so," the dragon said. "You wouldn't get *me* near one of those things! I suppose you've come for the Holy of Holies, Most Precious of Precious?"

"I have! And I intend to get it, too!"

"Don't be hasty with that thing," the dragon said in a worried tone. "You can *have* the Holy of Holies—just don't get near me with that damn magic sword." And so saying, he stepped aside without the slightest degree of reluctance or hesitation.

Yassun Dede hobbled past the dragon and into the courtyard of the castle. He entered the main hall and found himself in a great dark stone-walled passageway lighted with torches held by carved arms and hands, placed at regular intervals along the hall.

Suddenly he could see at the other end of the passageway a huge squat hairy troll standing at the ready with a battle-ax in his great bulbous hands, his huge balloon-like head hunched onto his shoulders, his short thick neck pulsing with blood rushing with adrenalin. He was a formidable enemy.

Yassun Dede brandished his sword, while balancing carefully on one leg and supporting himself with the hastily improvised crutch.

But because he was not used to having only one foot, the sword slipped as he rocked to one side, and the right ear was by chance sliced off clean to the jaw. As with the first two accidents, this wound also healed instantly.

"It doesn't matter," he muttered, half to himself and half to the walls, "when I am rich, I will get another of ivory, and anyone who wants to say anything to me will just have to talk to me from the left side, that's all." And he proceeded to hobble toward the troll.

"Looks like you have a magic sword there," the troll observed. "Yep—I can see by your ear that I was right. You get away from me with that damn thing!" And so saying, he ran off into the darkness of a side passageway.

"Now the whole castle will no doubt be alerted!" Yassun said to himself. "I had better be careful. Nonetheless, nothing can persuade me now to give up my quest when I am this close to success! I'd rather go down fighting to the last breath than be a hog-farmer again!"

He went on through the castle, encountering many dangerous enemies, but as soon as they saw the magic sword they ran away. And by and by he came to the base of a tower.

There before him was the bottom of a very steep circular stairway. He put his crutch on the lowest stair, and peered upward into the gloom. He saw nothing above him but more stairs, and yet he knew instinctively that above him somewhere was the Holy of Holies, Precious of Precious.

The stairs were bitter cold, dismal, and foreboding, but in his exultation it seemed to him like the stairway to heaven. With the help of his sword and his wooden crutch he was able to ascend slowly, step by step.

After a while he stopped to catch his breath for a few moments. The air was thick and moist, and he felt as if he had been carrying a heavy weight on his shoulders.

After some more climbing he came to a small window cut deeply into the stone. He leaned over and peered out. He could see nothing outside the castle, and the cold air of the outside struck his face and chilled the sweat running down over his cheeks. He could hear a low rumbling sound now, coming from above. At first it seemed to him like the thrumming of a huge heart, and then it sounded like a low chuckle of insane laughter.

After hearing this sound, Yassun Dede became suddenly more serious. For the first time during this adventure he began to consider the possibility that he had gotten himself into something far beyond his comprehension.

The climb upward became more difficult with each step. He was forced to stop every few minutes in order to rest and to breathe. Invisible fingers gripped themselves around his chest, squeezing his heart and choking his lungs. But the determination of his powerful aim held him, and he never once dreamed of turning back.

At last, when he thought that he could not possibly go any further, he came to a room at the top of the tower. A great, thick, oaken door barred the way. Heavy iron hinges and a huge iron lock prevented him from opening it, but he knew with every fiber of his being that behind that door lay the prize—the Holy of Holies, Most Precious of Precious.

He unsheathed the magic sword once more, and bent its fury upon the stout oak barrier. It took all his remaining strength to batter the door into a thousand pieces, and it now lay open to him. Behind him he could hear the mutterings, growls, and curses of hundreds of trolls, ogres, and bog-wolves who had been alerted and were coming now to the attack. They clattered and fell over one another as they clambered up the stone steps of the tower.

With his last hope gone, and with all the remaining effort of his depleted body, Yassun Dede crashed through the doorway into the tower room.

"I will somehow get through even this," he promised himself. "And the moment I take possession of the Holy of Holies, the Most Precious Precious, I will . . .Now, where is it?" He said. Turning quickly, before the first of the army of ogres and trolls burst through the open door, he had just enough time to quickly glimpse . . . the biggest razor back hog he had ever seen.

The "giant" sat back and roared with laughter when he saw that I had been buying it all along. I sat suddenly upright with my expression held in stupified disbelief. My jaw hung open, my eyes bugged out, my cheeks were a shade of scarlet. The giant rolled around on the floor, his teeth clacking as he shook with laughter. His straight straw-like hair flapped in rhythm with his giggling.

"I gotcha! I gotcha!" he cackled, barely able to gulp enough air to breathe.

"It wasn't *that* funny," I said, snatching up a spare singing harp and a dozen golden eggs to assuage my hurt feelings, disappointment and anger, and turned to leave the way I had come.

Or that is, I made every effort to leave, but which way had I come? A landscape made of nothing but clouds is pretty easy to get lost in if you are trying to get somewhere, because in that kind of landscape, anywhere you are is nowhere.

I had an idea to trace my path back from the face of the castle, but when I got a few yards away, and looked back at it, I realized that all four sides were the same. I remembered a trick for determining direction using sand-dunes, but I couldn't apply it to clouds.

As soon as I came to the full realization that I was lost, I began to apply the techniques I had learned as a woodsman in the Appalachian Mountains. That is, I began to run around in circles, yelling for help. As it happened — and mind you, I am telling you all this exactly as it *did* happen—I came by chance to a small break in the cloud surface, against the side of which someone had placed a ladder leading down to a patch of land on which sat a very tall snail. He began following my approach with his eyestalks as I descended the last few steps and walked over to where he sat.

"Who. . .Are. . .You. . .?" he asked. Ah, but I just remembered my promise to you. I said that I would not try to foist off the story of Alice in Wonderland on you, and here I almost did it without half realizing it.

CHAPTER FOURTEEN

THE SNAIL'S STORY

"Would you care to hear a story?" the snail asked.

"Certainly," I said. "I'm always in the market for a good story."

And I sat down politely in snail fashion. I only braced myself when he mentioned the title of the story, but after that I managed to recover sufficiently to listen to the rest of it.

In order to show the maximum amount of respect, as I had been taught to manifest outwardly toward all strangers, no matter how strange they were, I made no outward sign of confusion or concern other than the few slight automatic jerking motions caused by certain emotional factors, which were, due to his story, no longer under my intentional control.

"I am going to tell you the story of Yassun Dede And The Hollow Hill," he announced brightly. "Once upon a time there lived in a small hamlet in Denmark, a coppersmith by the name of Yassun Dede, who was a short blond fellow with bright blue eyes and a protruding chin."

"Au contraire," I stopped him. "Yassun Dede was a hog farmer," I pointed out.

"Don't interrupt, son. And he was the best damn coppersmith in the world. He could fix or make anything out of copper, tin, or brass."

"Well, then, why didn't they call him a tinsmith, or a brasssmith?" I asked.

"Hmph. He went around the countryside with his big pack in which he carried all his tools and scrap, and traveled from village to village. Since he was on the road most of the time, he was seldom at home in his cottage. So it didn't surprise him too much to find that a young lady in a princess costume had taken occupancy.

"It's not what you think," she explained. Well, Yassun was a slow thinker, and hadn't had time to come to any conclusion yet. In fact, he wasn't thinking about anything except his dinner, after carrying that heavy pack all over the countryside for a fortnight and a half.

"I'm hungry," he said. "Let's eat first, and then we'll see what I think and what I don't think."

The young lady fidgeted for a moment or two, and then asked plaintively, "You *are* the famous coppersmith, Yassun Dede?"

Yassun, now that he had had time to look at her carefully, would have said so even if he hadn't been. His answer must have satisfied her, because in a trice she was in the kitchen busily preparing a whopping meal for the two of them.

"I hope you like peanut butter," she said.

"Why?" asked Yassun.

"Because it's the only soup I know how to make." She said that with such a cute and winsome smile that Yassun didn't have the heart to say anything. He just grinned and nodded like a hula girl in the back of an automobile.

When they had finished their meal of peanut butter soup, the young girl began her story:

"I am the daughter of a very powerful king, whose realm extends over the land known as the *Takavorbas Empire*. Not long ago something terrible happened to our kingdom, something which only a coppersmith—the best coppersmith in the world—would be able to correct. My father sent me here to find you and bring you with me to our land, for it is well known that you are the best coppersmith in the entire world."

"Aw, shucks," said Yassun, trying his best to appear humble, but failing utterly to seem less than "excitedly in agreement with her opinion of him". "Never mind all that. . .wanna mess around?"

"Please, Mr. Dede, I had to travel in disguise and find you without really telling anyone what I was up to. They would kill us both if they found us together."

"Who would?" Yassun asked, now suddenly concerned. "You think they would do anything to hurt me? It's you they're after, isn't it?" he asked in a worried tone. "You better leave before they find you. . .I'm concerned only for your safety, of course."

Suddenly there was a thumping and scraping sound at the window. The light went out and the room was pitched into darkness. Realizing the possible danger, Yassun choked back a sudden impulse to ask "Where was Moses when the light went out?"

"Good thinking, young lady," Yassun said. "They can't see us in here if the light's out."

"I didn't blow the light out," she said in a quavering voice.

"Well if you didn't blow out the light, and I didn't blow out the light, who the hell blew out the light?" Yassun said in a high-pitched hysterical voice.

"I did," said a strange foreign voice, and at that moment a match was struck.

In the light Yassun and the girl could see the stranger who had relit the lamp. He seemed to be very old, but he had the grace of a young man. He had a long white beard, snow-white hair, great bushy eyebrows that stuck way out from his forehead, and he wore a long white robe. He carried a staff in his hand, which he used as a walking stick. He strode quickly across the room and settled in the overstuffed chair in front of the hearth.

"Yassun Dede, the famous coppersmith?"

Yassun was getting irritated. He had hoped for a little more time in which to overcome the girl's indecision regarding messing around.

Still, he answered civilly, first because he realized that had the stranger meant them any harm, he would have already done something, and secondly and not unimportantly, his parents had trained him to always have good manners toward elders no matter what. In fact, had the old man been a murderer, he still would have been polite to him in spite of everything.

"Yes, I am Yassun Dede," he replied with some degree of apprehension discernable in his shaking voice.

"Who are you? What do you want with us?" asked the girl in a terrified voice. "How did you know we were here?"

"It is my business to know these things," the old stranger replied. "I am known as—Gandalf the White."

"Okay," I stopped the snail. "You don't have to go any further. . . What do you mean, throwing Gandalf into that story? Haven't you any integrity?" ·

The snail pulled himself up to his full ten-foot height, eyestalks waving wildly. "Bah!" he shouted. "What do you expect from a ten-foot tall snail?"

I realized that once again, I had been had. Finishing my small repast of *escargot*, I again went on my way to find a path home.

CHAPTER FIFTEEN

THE FROG'S STORY

In just a short while I came to a small lake upon which was an island. A gondolier was rowing his gondola around and around in circles near the shore.

"Where does the signore wish to go?" he asked.

"I suppose Detroit would be too much to ask. . .?" I replied.

He took me over to the island, and I walked to the center to see if there was any way back to the earth over there. It was that or walk around on clouds back upstairs the rest of the day. Thanks to my snail friend I was no longer hungry, but it would have been nice to top it off with a pizza.

"Do you know anyone who delivers?" I asked the gondolier, but he was already halfway across the lake.

I discovered a stone stairway leading down into the island, and naturally I went down there to see what was in there. And the only reason I took such a risk was because a certain feeling was growing within me, slowly taking over my entire presence, which could be constated as "If I see one more acre of clouds today I am going to scream indefinately."

The stairway opened into a large room, at one end of which was a carved stone throne. The room was lighted with torches thrust out from the stone walls. I often wondered how they keep those things lighted for years after these places have been abandoned, like in *Abbott and Costello Meet The Wolf Man.*

But the room was not entirely abandoned, as I could see when I made the adjustment to the dim light. On the ground just to the right of the throne sat a giant green frog dressed in a neat gray pinstriped business suit.

"All right," he said. "Do you want to hear my story or don't you?"

"I'm not sure," I answered. "You start in, and I'll stop you if I can't take it."

"Fair enough," he said. "There was once a land which rose high above the seas, past the Pillars of Herakles, and in this once-famous country lived a great poet, the illuminated Yassun Dede."

"I suppose," I interrupted, "that it will do me no good whatever, to point out that, on the contrary, Yassun Dede was the most miserable hogfarmer that ever lived?"

". . . And this Yassun Dede the poet one day consulted the oracle, who foretold that the once-great poet would someday become a simple hog-farmer and live far from the shores of that Blessed Realm."

". . .And I suppose it would do just as little good to mention," I added, "that he was not a hog-farmer after all, but a coppersmith?"

". . . And then, according to the oracle, Yassun Dede would become a coppersmith and live in a castle with a beautiful princess. . . "

"Just a minute," I told the frog. "I am beginning to become something of an expert on this Yassun Dede, and I happen to know that the story you are about to tell me is going to be a real dud. I just know you are going to shaft it to me, and I am determined not to be had again by one of these Yassun Dede stories. So I'll tell you what I'm going to do. I'm going to. . ."

"Grab your ass," said the frog.

"Grab my ass, and. . . Who said that?"

"Hiya, Hiya, Hiya," croaked the frog as he disappeared with a peculiar twanging sound. All that remained was a puff of smoke.

"Too bad," I mused. "I had just got my heart set on frog's legs."

CHAPTER SIXTEEN

MY OWN STORY

And now, dear reader, I will tell you a story of my own, not relating anything about Yassun Dede. And if you fully believe this, I have some Indian land on the shores of the Colorado River that I'd just love to sell to you.

There was once a small official—not over five feet tall—who lived in a town near the Meander River and who had obtained, through massive doses of blackmail and bribery, the post of Health Inspector Of Restaurants. There were only two restaurants in town, but he made it his business to make the job as complicated as possible.

He would inspect the restaurants every single day, rain or shine—taking the morning to inspect one, and the afternoon to inspect the other, of course sampling every item on the menu to insure its safety for the public health.

He was very concerned about the public's health, in particular regarding food poisoning resulting from the ingestion of bad wine and cognac, and so he took especial care to sample at least once a day every item in stock in that all-important category.

It seemed from his immediate prospects that he would remain at that post all the rest of his life, as the only other job that could be obtained through blackmail and bribery was that of Postmaster, and only two people in town could read, and only one of those could write, although no one on earth could read his writing. The same fellow who could write was also the local interpreter. He spoke 87 different languages, but none of them could be identified.

And since the Health Inspector was not either one of these two educated persons, he could not hope to hold the post of chief letter writer, the Postmaster. Besides, you can't eat the mail. So he kept on at the job of Inspector of Restaurants for some years. . . as a matter of fact, until his youth had been almost entirely forgotten.

Suddenly he heard a mysterious voice that seemed to come from inside his head. The strange voice commanded him to quit his job immediately and walk to the river nearby, and wait there for further instructions.

"All right," he sighed. "I knew something like this was going to happen sooner or later. I've gone crazy, that's all there is to it. Might as well do as the voice says. I've been working too hard. I need a vacation anyway."

As soon as he gave notice on his job there were seventy one applications for the position, and the battle raged so heavily that no one noticed him as he wandered away.

He went to the river and waited for the voice to come again. Suddenly it spoke in a loud, crisp commanding tone.

"Tear off all your clothes and jump into the river."

And that's what he did. Ripping off all his clothes, he jumped into the swift current of the river. But instead of drowning, as most people would have, he just drifted on the stream for a long time. Finally a fisherman managed to haul him over the side of his boat.

"What are you trying to do, drown yourself?" the man asked. "The current is too strong in this river for you to try to swim!"

"To tell you the truth," he said to the fisherman, "I don't know what I'm doing. A voice told me to strip off all my clothes and jump into the river, and that's what I did."

The fisherman took him in, and gave him some dry clothes, food, and a place to sleep. Days turned to weeks, and weeks turned to months. But one day he heard the voice again. It told him to leave the fisherman immediately and walk along the road. He jumped up and ran out to the road, and began walking.

After only a little while, a farmer came riding up on his wagon. "Hey, I need a hand with my harvesting!" he said.

"Okay," he said, and worked for the farmer for several months before he heard the voice again.

"Get up right this minute and walk to the nearest city."

"But I haven't finished milking this goat yet," he said.

"Are you going to follow my instructions, or aren't you?"

"Yes, of course I am. . ." he said, getting up and leaving without even removing the milking pail from underneath the goat.

When he got there, the voice came to him again.

"Now take your savings and invest it in furs."

So he took the little he had saved from his time with the fisherman and the farmer, and invested it in furs. He became very rich and very successful. But one day he heard the mysterious voice again.

"Give everything away and become a beggar, trusting only in God to provide everything you need."

And so that is what he did. But after several years on the road, he ended up near death, painfully starved and his body wrecked from a series of beatings at the hands of fearful or spiteful villagers.

At last he lay under a tree, dying and alone, suffering unimaginable physical and mental tortures. Suddenly, the voice, which had been silent all these years, came to him again.

"How is it going?" asked the voice.

"I'm dying of starvation, illness and broken bones, and you ask how it's going? This is all happening to me just because you told me to give up everything and become a beggar and trust in you to provide."

"Shmuck," said the voice. *"Who told you to listen to me?"*

CHAPTER SEVENTEEN

THE INNER WORLD

How has it come to this? Why cannot that "complete sensing of myself" remain with me even now, when the mental part of my being, the psyche, has closed down during this accident?

Can it be possible that my consciousness, which always used to manifest in the best interests of beings everywhere, and which was attained by me through continual effort and special kinds of suffering, is now about to vanish forever without a trace, just when its presence is more important for humanity than even the atmosphere of the earth?

No, of course not. It will not happen in that way, according to everything I have learned about Objective Justice. But still, something is happening. . .Hmmm—I seem to be continuing to exist at least in Essence—my objectively formed consciousness has not yet entirely dissipated.

Of course, I have for many billenia now, worked unceasingly for the common good of all beings, and therefore this consciousness of mine must have remained intact just out of sheer habit, in spite of the accident which has just occurred to the body.

It must continue! It is especially necessary more than ever, when I have just recently been given the means with which I can provide all the data and techniques required for the attainment of real awakening in humans, which is more important to them than just their transitory happiness in the material world!

This supernatural inner conversation took place within my inner world on the morning of October 30, 1949, as I sat in the Night Owl Cafe in Greenwich Village, almost as if those ideas had been implanted in me by another completely different source of active thought.

It could not have been my own thoughts, I realized, rubbing my abdomen absent-mindedly. Of course it might be simply that I was working too hard. I had not slept at all well during the previous week in which I had worked literally feverishly, with a body temperature of one hundred and three degrees, on my book, and the high fever which I had been more or less ignoring for the past ten days had become worse this morning, and I finally had agreed to go see a doctor, later that day.

This was further irritated by the continuous efforts I had been making in spite of a bout of insomnia of the past several months caused by the conflict arising in me by the apparently impossible problem with which I was now faced.

I had taken with myself a firm and solemn vow—not like the casual oaths usually taken by Americans which can be broken ten minutes later without a single twinge of conscience—to publish or at least complete for future publication the book which was to become *The American Book of the Dead,* containing the method for conscious travel through the between lives states, and also for those who study deeply, the method for attaining real awakening, and conscious life.

Readings of the manuscript of the book of transit instructions were held in our apartment on 14th Street in New York, until late September of 1949, when the fever began, and my health broke to a serious degree.

At the same time, I had gotten the sudden impression that no one understood any of it. Whenever we got to certain passages, they would promptly fall asleep on the floor as if they had been given knockout drops, and afterward they remembered nothing of the incident.

From these reactions I was able to develop the technique of using applied stress to break down the psyche and expose the Essence, but at the same time, it was too powerful to use with just anyone, particularly readers who had not been prepared for such reactions in themselves.

It finally became obvious to me that every phrase, every paragraph, and every word of the manuscript would have to be rewritten in order to make it usable for the public in a general edition. I could not have everyone who casually read that material faint away, perhaps in the middle of traffic or around machinery.

But just at the time when I had come to this realization, there arose before me the specter of the limited duration of my life here on earth. It was obvious now that if the existing version of the American Book of the Dead had taken only one year to write, then the rewrite—which would have to be tested for harmlessness—would take at least four or five years to complete under ordinary circumstances.

And an additional problem arose, in that the exercises and gym techniques needed to be introduced along with the new material, which in its public form would be only largely theoretical, without its previous power to knock out the everyday consciousness cold at the points where the individual ordinarily blacked out during the transit state between death and rebirth.

But where could I possibly find the time to do all this? If I myself controlled the subjective flow of time within my own inner world consciousness, and also within the organism, I could expect to complete the task in only a few months, and then I could live my life in peace, and eventually die in a satisfied state, knowing that I had introduced the Teaching into the ordinary life of humans on earth and that it could now become a practical aspect of ordinary existence.

But it just so happened that it was not under my control, as I had arranged previously, for other quite different reasons, to have the job taken over completely by the Office of Cosmic Coincidence Control, specifically to the Archangel Michael, and so there now remained for me only a very definite span of time in which to complete my labors among humans on earth, and which was now completely unchangeable by me and to which I had to concur.

But it was not just a whim of mine that I had become a constant participant in the final hours on earth of so many candidates for the world to come—not only because of this book about death and rebirth, but also because I had already formulated certain methods according to the oral tradition already existing, and wished to test its efficient use in tracking individuals through the death states and back into rebirth or through transformation into the higher realms beyond existence.

But because of all these frantic preparations to complete my work before death overtook me in the midst of my efforts toward all beings everywhere, the organs in my body, which had up to that time been quite friendly with each other, suddenly aroused in themselves a real hatred for their blood brothers and sisters, and as a result had cut all helpful communication between themselves.

Considering all the punishment endured so far by the organism during all these and subsequent efforts I made to bring this work to completion, I am not at all surprised that the body reacted in this way. And also, one must consider besides all that the strange *power* which haunts all conscious efforts toward humans, and for whose existence, I—and I alone—am curiously responsible.

It was perhaps just this same peculiar force which nearly destroyed me and my work forever several times during my life through the action upon the organism of almost mortal injury. Even these "coincidental injuries" should have each been sufficient in themselves to have put the *coup de grace* to my efforts among humans on the planet earth long ago.

The first of these "strange coincidences" occurred in 1956 during the troubles in Cuba. I had sailed there with a friend just for a weekend caper, so to speak. We left the coast of Florida and landed near Havana in order to meet my friend's family, all of whom were later shot and killed by pro-Castro forces, since they were pro-Battista. But as we left the house following lunch, I was suddenly struck by a stray bullet coming from nowhere.

They got me into the back of their Buick and drove me to a doctor somewhere in the city. When my consciousness returned to the body, I was not only able to describe what had happened as if seen from above, but I was also able to predict for others certain events in their lives, and to see past events in their lives quite easily—although I was never able to do this for myself. This new ability came so surprisingly that I had no idea how to apply it or what it could be used for. It did not occur to me to explore it further at that time.

During my time out of the body I had been shown through several spaces by two guides, who only gave me permission to return to earth if I undertook a journey to several places in which I would be given knowledge for the use of others and which I was to share as quickly as possible and with as many people as possible. I did not really wish to remain out of the earth area at that time, because I felt some responsibility to other humans to bring what I had learned to their attention. After all, it was only accident that led me to discover the completely alien spaces that were available outside the human world.

After two solid weeks of wandering around the jungles of Yucatan, near Merida, through literally impassable tourist traps set up at intervals among the foliage, and having found nothing useful in the ancient ruins—useful for my quest upon which I had been sent by the guides—with my health still not completely recovered from the gunshot wound, superficial as it was, many unusual visitors, native to the warm jungle climate, were able to implant themselves within my organism due to the extreme vulnerability caused by the aforementioned wound. They later were able to demonstrate without doubt their continued habitation and chronic existence within my body through the performance of several of their rituals, called *malaria* and *encephalitis,* both of which I survived.

At the same time other gourmets of the human body had come to sample the outer covering of the organism in order to enjoy the savory taste of the said human meat and internal liquid refreshment so loved by mosquitoes and fruit flies, which said internal liquid normally served the function of conveying oxygen, nitrogen and carbon dioxide along with other specific trace elements in a more or less circular system around the planetary body.

And moreover the doses in which they took the said refreshments were so minute and so quietly did they partake of their repast that it was a full week before I noticed that anything was missing.

I was honored also with the opportunity to provide a modest hospitality to still other guests taking up temporary and permanent residence in the organism as well.

Through the necessity of involuntarily ingesting foods prepared in, or resulting from, rancid oils and fats, I enjoyed the company of gout.

And through other equally involuntary actions on my part resulting from necessities arising in the jungle, these visitors also included *mononucleosis, hypoglycemia,* and also, due to my rigidly vegetarian diet, thanks to a certain amount of squeamishness regarding unusual life forms and the ingestion of organisms similar to my own, which I have since then managed to overcome almost completely, I contracted the illness—really not an illness at all, but a dietary problem—called *pernicious anemia.*

During the period of recuperation from all this, after having left the jungle weaker but no wiser, I was subjected to many other formidable illnesses which had for ages past been the scourge of humanity. Among these were the dreaded *Ashikarkian Bardk, Charaji'ji Meghuapuys',* and *Aylantag Harutiun,* all of which have left more or less permanent scars upon my being to commemorate their visits with me.

And even though I eventually recovered from these things, the organism never fully erased all traces of these invasions, which even now appear chronically even under the best of conditions.

Some time passed during which I had at least some relief from these reminders of my vulnerable existence while in a human form, but not too long passed before another catastrophe was dumped upon this already quite tampered with organism manifested by me here on earth.

In the year 1963 another of these lead projectiles loved by and almost worshipped by men on earth managed to burrow its way into my body by falling rather quickly through the outer covering called "skin".

This second "coincidental shooting" took place while I drove my Morgan Plus Four spruce-framed automobile into a crowd of very envious beings called "highway robbers" in the mountains near Asmara, Ethiopia.

I was shot simply because I would not stop to allow them to relieve me of my means to leave the country—that is to say, my passport and money. I was only able to escape this recurring destiny of mine because of the presence of a medical officer of American armed forces origin who rode with me, and was able to apply field emergency procedures.

During the next month I again encountered the guides as my consciousness drifted in and out of coma. I was taken to a planet which had been completely destroyed and burned out. They told me that this was going to happen to the earth, and that it had happened before, when the planet had passed through clouds of luminous gases which had become incandescent upon contact with the earth.

In this period I learned the basic methods for breaking down the psyche, and began to understand the construction of the Essence, and how it survives death and maintains the basic identity through preservation of habits and tendencies. At the same time, I gained the disquieting ability to direct physical objects and bodies from any distance, and to communicate without having to use a body for speech and hearing.

It was this recurring situation of alternate periods of delirium and unconsciousness to which both my friends and my most respected and admired enemies have attributed much of my writing ideas and teaching techniques.

During the next few years, I learned to control the powers which had been aroused in me during this series of interviews with the guide, and through continual practice was able to bring them to a peak.

But suddenly the third "coincidental shooting" occurred during a visit to the Superstition Mountains in December of 1968. This third—and I hope last—coincidental stray bullet struck my back only an inch from the spinal column. I had been shot, as I found out later, by a Yaqui Indian for, as usual, trespassing on sacred ground—or so I was told.

Just as this third bullet struck my body, a companion of mine grabbed me and realizing that I had been shot, wrestled me aboard a donkey, thinking that we would soon feel the results of further projectiles if we remained there any longer.

I was far out of the local space by this time, once again with the two guides, while my companion led the donkey further into the mountain as the way back to Apache Junction was now blocked by rifle fire.

He took us away from the First Water Ranch, toward Willow Spring through O'Grady Canyon, hoping to circle around through Black Mesa and down to the highway.

But it soon became obvious that I would not be able to continue, and that he would have to go alone for help. As I found out later, he returned the same evening with a medical aide from Phoenix, but by the time they arrived at the cave where he had left me, I was no longer inside it.

While all this was going on I had come to for a few moments and could tell that I had been carried off somewhere into a deeper and larger cavern. I caught a glimpse of an Apache just before I blacked out again.

Later when my consciousness returned to the body, I could see many mummified remains of former inhabitants of the planet sitting propped up against the back walls.

In my feverish state I thought they were alive, seated in deep reverie while observing the progression of the ages of the earth, in mutual harmony with the planet and with each other. This was my first impression of them as I lay there partly conscious and partly delirious. Delirium was getting to be with me a more or less regular state of affairs.

I remained there in that cavern under the care of the man who had found me and, thinking I had been abandoned, had brought me there almost two weeks before.

The life and death struggle for domination of my organism, on the one hand for the continuation of my efforts toward humanity, and on the other, for the use of the planet as fertilizer, began in earnest as I lay there half in one world and half in the other.

After only a few days my consciousness reluctantly returned to the body sufficiently for me to be able to scrabble about in the cavern like a sick land-crab. In my only partly reconstructed psyche, I began to believe that my immortal companions at the rear of the cave had invited me to share their tea-luncheon during which they discussed the wisdom of the ages—to which I had become somehow privy, especially to the secrets of life, death, and the eternal struggle against the flow of time.

And in this delirium of mine, I came to believe that they were my teachers and that I was learning from the Secret Chiefs all the inner mysteries of life beyond the material world.

Finally, when I felt well enough to walk without much pain, I realized that none of this had any meaning whatever, and left the cave. The man who had nursed me back to health did not offer to come with me, and probably felt that I was now quite able to care for myself. I was not far from civilization, and could make it back without too much struggle.

He was indeed a great friend, who helped me to heal myself but did not insist that I remain in good health from that moment on, just to insure that his time had not been wasted, as so many healers do.

You can easily imagine the surprise of everyone when I casually walked in at the ranch, having been lost up in the mountain for over two weeks. Because of the rugged terrain, air searches are usually considered futile. They had simply assumed when I did not come back that I had joined the hundreds of dead who had been eaten by the mountain at one time or another.

Superstition Mountain is located east of Phoenix, Arizona, in the Western United States, and more or less to the south of the Painted Desert and the Grand Canyon. The air up there seems to me to be the most vivifying on the planet, and maybe even elsewhere. This place seemed at the time to be the mixing crucible in which the atmospheres of heaven and hell combine before becoming the tepid and mediocre atmosphere humans are used to having in order to breathe.

In the midst of the mountain itself, nothing of any kind grows except an occasional scrub desert bush or a hardy sprout, and one cannot find much water, except in pot-holes in the rock, where rainwater—if any—collects.

And so I walked painfully—but not too painfully—downward toward civilization across this great sprawling pile of hot stone which profoundly resembled in my opinion the combined efforts of hell, and as I walked, or actually stumbled, there slowly began to be aroused in me that chronic condition of delirium once again during which a little idea began to arise in my thoughts which when it became a full-blown *idea,* altered completely my state of being and gave a new meaning to the word Essence. Moreover, it made unnecessary all the efforts to remain awake which I had been making up to then at unbelievable cost to my energy state.

As I wandered down the mountain, and had gone as far as Crockett Springs, I think, I found some water in a hole. And rather than chance drinking it, I poured it over my head, allowing it to drip down over my shoulders.

Suddenly, about five minutes later, my body became weak and numb, and I found my legs folding up under me so that I ended up sitting cross-legged on the ground. I sat there for some time.

My body had seemed to dissipate into the still hot air, and I recall wondering at that moment whether or not I still had a body. Once again a thought came to me which had occurred before only during the times I had been recovering from the accidental shootings, but now it was quite clear to me, perhaps again due to my condition of partial delirium. Up to then this thought had only been dimly perceived by me, but now I could very definitely state it as a complete idea.

How about that? It seems that I've lived through another one. Does this mean that I am going to have to keep on going in the same old way? I have all these powers, and yet I am continually regretful at the emptiness of it all. How can I possibly do any more than I have already to create in myself the awakened state?

I have managed to increase my mental powers over material things and other people far beyond anything dreamed of by occultists and scholars, and I have all this while remained merciless to the weaknesses and desires of my human part, in order to not fall accidentally into unconsciousness and psyche encapsulation caused by identification with the fleeting forms of consciousness, thoughts, emotions and sensations of this organism.

But in spite of all this, even though I could now cause a cow to drop to the ground at five hundred feet, or walk upon clouds and appear to anyone anywhere in the world—or out of it—I cannot manage to maintain in myself full Essence consciousness during a period of stress, without manifesting some old habit or other not at all appropriate to conscious life.

Apparently, my Essence depends for its existence at least in the open upon the state of the body, and so my consciousness is worth exactly nothing.

Even with my powers I cannot prevent unconsciously accumulated habits from taking over the moment that the body comes under a stress condition.

And just when my organism is subjected to stress, the psyche is forced from the control of consciousness into a closed-down condition, while my habits take over, and I am a bundle of sheer reaction while the organism is directed by the ever-surviving body of habits.

Each time an emergency occurs, and after the initial shock of reaction has passed, the habitual thoughts begin to pass through in all their glory: the habit to survive through food, the habit to survive through identity, the habit to survive through sex, the habit to survive through being human, the habit to survive through objects, and so forth.

And while all this is going on, the passions and aggressions of survival can be felt as emotional sensations: pride, envy, jealousy, hatred, vanity, and protective love of the psyche—all flowing from somewhere, the source being apparently bottomless and endless.

And even though I have fought terrible battles within myself over this, and I have searched everywhere in the world and out of it among not only the wise, but also among the simple for an answer, I have not yet found the solution to this problem.

If only I could have a life completely free from any outside distractions, I would be able to maintain the control of the organism through the psyche continually, thus being able to manifest myself in accordance with my wishes.

But if I am to be forced continually to confront outer world people and objects in constantly changing situations, I am doomed to experience only ordinary consciousness every time the body or the mind are subjected to some stress or other, compelling the essence to take over. There must be a way to replace these unconscious habits which have accumulated over the past millions of years—and which have up to now been my real self, surviving whole and untouched the stresses of death and rebirth—with new, conscious habits, which would create in me a new real self which had the habit of living conscious life, and when exposed by stress would still reflect my full consciousness and spirit.

They must be replaced, because I already know that they cannot be eliminated. They are, after all, my deepest self— that part of me which survives everything and which becomes more or less a traveling spore of consciousness and identity during the between lives state.

But what can I do to make this happen? I have tried everything I could think of to make my essence behave. But no matter what I have done, nothing was effective for very long. Even if at first these reminding factors were cathartic, I soon got used to them, and then they had no effect at all.

This seems to be an endless knot, and the more I pull on the strings, the tighter it gets.

But wait! Here is an idea I have never seen before. . .this strange and powerful idea is intruding itself into my awareness, and. . .How simple it is! How obvious it is! Of all the thoughts that have previously passed through my consciousness and of all the other thoughts which I had aroused deliberately, why had this never occurred to me before?

Why have I forced myself to suffer so deeply over this, and compelled myself to pass through states caused by gunshot wounds before I could accept this simple thought?

All I need to do, in order to form a completely new essence, is to create continual severe stress for myself for the remainder of my life, thus never allowing the psyche to control the organism. And while the essence is continually exposed, it can be altered in accordance with a perpetually conscious life!

But how can I create constant stress around myself, every single moment of every single day for the rest of my life and if possible for the remainder of my existence as a being, even through eternity? What could possibly be so constant and unfailing? I know that I cannot perform this task for myself. I have tried before to do this, and I have forgotten here and there to maintain it.

Now I have an even bigger problem than I had before, because I know what needs to be done, and I know why it has to be this way, but I don't know how to make it happen. I already know from long experience that it just doesn't happen by itself. One must consciously choose the path of stress, or the Path of Struggle—and one cannot maintain the battle against oneself by oneself; help of some kind is needed.

But wait—I know that some beings have received help of this kind before, because I can see that there are individuals who are always acting from essence—who never have traces of the psyche present in their daily lives. How did they do it? What kind of help did they get?

And another problem suddenly strikes me. Is the essence, composed as it is of eighteen basic habits—and only eighteen are possible to contain in the essence—sufficient for daily needs? Will I still be able to continue my life and relationships after I have let go of the complicated and interesting psyche, and am left with the simple and direct thoughts and emotions—and extremely direct actions—of the essence?

Of course I will. There are many individuals who have managed to continue in this world even with only the essence with which to relate, to communicate and to work. But the problem still remains. . .How am I going to create constant and never-ending stress for myself, every moment, so that I can have an every-minute essence?

Aha! Of course! I am not the first to have this problem, by any means. Who did have this problem first? It may be that by seeing how it was solved before, I can solve it for myself. But I must have some lead, some little clue!

Of course! Of course! God was the first one to have this problem. Didn't He have a complete absence of all stress before creation? And didn't He create man in His own image? And if I exist—along with all His other creations—within the simulation of His inner world, which we experience as the outer world? Then that means that I have an inner and outer world existing as exact analogies to His inner and outer worlds. That must mean that my inner and outer worlds have the exact same characteristics as His! And there's my answer!

This answers the question that has plagued humans for thousands of years! Why did God deliberately create the Devil? Was there a use for him?

All that has ever been shown about God is that He is all-good, all powerful, and absolutely just. Then why did He, in His loving mercy and compassion, give life and power to His beloved son Lucifer, the Prince of Light, and then cast him off into the outer darkness, bestowing upon him a power almost equal to, but opposite from, His own—and at the same time place a curse upon his beloved son, that he could never return to the throne?

Now, suddenly, I know why God consciously created the Devil! And why the old magician had offered to show me how to create "a debil" of my own!

Yes, even God had been compelled to create and give power to the Office of the Devil, simply because even He falls into periods of sleep and awakening, and even He is in essence nothing more than habits—although very great habits, such as the habit to create a universe, and the habit to redeem the souls within it—and He needs to maintain a steady essence-state or the entire universe would fall into unconsciousness.

I realize now that the Lord must have very early in creation arrived at this solution just as I have now arrived at the same solution. I must create for myself a perpetual and self-initiating "outside force" which will constantly apply stress to my being, whether I remember it or not, and whether I wish it or not. Moreover, it must be so fanatic in this that it never lets up, not even for one instant!

Now all that remains for me to do is to find within myself something which corresponds to His beloved son, and cast it into the outer world forever to serve as a perpetual creator of stress, and thus to create in me a perpetual state of essence.

But what is there in myself that is so vital to me that just because it exists apart from me it would be felt as a continual stress powerful enough to utterly and forever destroy the psyche? And what is powerful enough in there?

Oh. . .now I see it—and I am not so sure I like this one bit, now that I know what I must sacrifice. It is something which I have built up in myself only after long and hard suffering and effort, and which I have labored over for years to polish, and to refine. It is something which I have nurtured with more striving and care than anything ever before done by me. And yet it is the only thing that is powerful enough, and yes. . .it would definitely cause in me a continual yearning, stress and suffering at least strong enough to permanently destroy my psyche—perhaps even to the point of insanity.

Yes, it would have to go. My Power Of Mind, which up to now has made life so easy for me that I have actually become more or less a spoiled brat through its continual use in making everything go right for me all the time, assuring me of a life in which no conflict whatever existed, regardless of the wishes of great nature and of other beings existing around me.

I had up to now in fact, through the use of this power, become as lazy and in some ways degraded and degenerate as that all-time notorious user of the same powers, the monk Rasputin.

I realize that if this power—my Holy of Holies, Most Precious of Precious—were ever driven away from me, I would be left as helpless as a virgin in a den of slave traders. I have come to depend on it so entirely that if I am forced to live without it, my life will be an endless round of extra and from this standpoint useless labor and defense against the forces of nature.

But there is no doubt about it. If cast out away from me, it would serve as a perpetual—if painful—reminder and source of stress. Its absence would without doubt constantly taunt me and tempt me to recover it in order to continue in the same easy effortless way as before.

What could cause more stress, or more powerful stress, than the sacrifice of one's firstborn son? Now I see clearly the parable of Abraham. . .And I don't like the prospect one bit.

And so, with only a moment's hesitation, I deliberately and consciously cast out my own beloved son—the power of telepathic hypnotism, and control over matter and energy, which I had developed within myself over so many years of hard work—into the outer darkness, never to return.

And ever since that exact moment in which I did this, its absence has never for a single moment failed to cause in me sheer anguish, compelling my psyche to remain forever disintegrated, causing as a result my continued conscious life here on earth. And since that moment I have felt both its suffering and mine as a result of its existence apart from me.

And with poignant rememberance, I can see him now—desperately striving to return, never comprehending the reason for his exile, not understanding what transgression he has made, never understanding the reason for his perpetual suffering at never, ever, being able to return to his father, always hoping somehow to be taken up into the light once again—and all this just for my benefit! Glory to him who makes it all possible, and gratitude for the great sufferer who could never be told his real use and purpose for existence.

And so, I have cast out the power which makes possible communication between the stars, the curing of cancer, the healing of the sick, and the raising of the dead—all for the attainment of conscious life, and for the eventual benefit of all life everywhere.

I fully realize the great respect with which my beloved son is held by humans, and that they all wish for his power. And in a way, they are quite right. This power must be fully accepted and developed in one before it can be cast out, for one cannot cast out what one does not have.

Only when it has become for one a real beloved son—only then is it time to cast it out. And that will be a terrible and painful sacrifice if it has really become for one a beloved child.

And during the period in which this power of mind over matter is being perfected in you, you can prepare to make the great sacrifice by practicing on smaller beloveds—just second cousins, aunts, uncles, and in-laws on a smaller scale. This will build up one's will so that when the time comes to make the real sacrifice, it will be almost possible to cast him into the outer darkness without more than a momentary hesitation.

These smaller scale beloveds upon which one can practice are the beloved relatives of the son, called *passions, aggressions, habitual self-pity, worry about what will become of one in the future, greed, desire for objects and people, lust, envy, pride, and jealousy.* You will not be fit for the main event unless you build up to it with these little favorite aunts of yours. If you cannot cast them out, you have no hope at all to cast out the favorite son, and it will take you over completely—then you will be stuck with all those powers and no way to get rid of them.

Now, thanks to this little idea of mine, it was no longer necessary to continue the self flagellation of mine, which up to then had been required in order to keep the essence exposed and the psyche down, thus keeping myself in a constantly awakened state.

The appearance of my beloved son everywhere around me has proved beyond any doubt that I have been succesful in detaching him from me, for he appears everywhere, manifesting his power in many ways.

What a stunning shock it was to see the many efforts of his on my behalf. I have managed to somehow justify all this by convincing myself that the people who have fallen under his domination are far beyond the reach of the work anyway, and that while working under his power they at least learn how to communicate and control the environment to the extent that they can add their own weight to his efforts on my behalf. Imagine that—all those people working just to keep me awake!

The years have dragged on slowly and all around me the definite signs of my beloved son's work on my behalf have become more and more evident. Thanks to him—and only to him—I have been able to drive myself into a regular tizzy of effort toward human beings and incidentally toward all other beings as well, and through this constant struggle, and because of it, I have been able to observe the inner essence world of humans whenever they came near me, thus attracting momentarily the fullness of his wrath and cunning by being in the target area for a while.

During this time I have been constrained, as a result of all the counter-efforts of my beloved son, and the resulting attraction to schools of power of most humans, to work with only a small group of pupils devoted to my ideas and who are happy living in the simplicity of the essence without the comfort of the psyche or the power.

Unfortunately, I have so far only discovered two dozen such individuals out of a possible several billion humans, but I am confident that there are at least a hundred more!

I have been periodically stripped of material support, but not, thank God, spiritual support. Always, defeat is replaced with indomitable hope and a sincere wish for the introduction of conscious life into the mainstream of humanity.

Once again my destiny has overcome all odds, and all because of this little idea—first invented by God, of course—of creating for myself an outside source of irritation and stress, forcing my psyche to self-destruct, and allowing my essence to remain and to rebuild itself along conscious lines of existence—all thanks to my beloved son, in whom I am well-pleased.

Soon, forces of his, always and in everything negating my efforts, were arrayed against me. I was compelled to take lodgings in a small apartment, and conduct meetings at a small office on an off-street in Hollywood, called the Cosmo Street office, which could be rented for only fifty dollars a month—and toward which I had little or no help for its maintenance. There I could introduce these ideas to anyone interested. When it became obvious that everyone who might have been interested had already enrolled in schools directed by my beloved son, I closed up the office and moved to the mountains.

This was in 1970, and it had become obvious to me by now that since all automatic material support had stopped for me at the moment I had cast out my beloved son, I would have to find some way of arousing material means for the establishment of at least one center in which this knowledge could be transmitted in the midst of unconscious life, or my work would be destroyed forever, and all this would have to be rediscovered later, more or less accidentally, by someone else.

And then I realized that in all probability this secret is periodically destroyed, thanks to the effective efforts of my beloved son, and that it has to be periodically rediscovered anyway. It must have existed many times in the past, only to be utterly destroyed by unconscious beings working for the beloved son, who without a single twinge of conscience, completely obliterate any trace of it which might have remained to guide others in the future.

And so I had the brainstorm of touring the countryside in order to explain and demonstrate some of these ideas and methods accidentally discovered by me. But we had only gone from Cowichan Center for Gestalt Learning in British Columbia—which I had been asked to direct, and did direct for a period of a year, during which time all hope of its continued existence died, and lynch mobs had gathered to run everyone out on a rail because I had simply introduced my ideas there instead of running the usual psyche-building exercise programs the community had come to expect—to Esalen in Big Sur, when we realized that we would never be able to reach anyone with these ideas directly. And so even our last few pennies, upon which our hopes had been to build some small capital for my work, went to my beloved son instead, to finance his work. And even though I knew that his work was all for my benefit—and I was grateful, believe me—I had hoped to spread that benefit to other individuals.

And so, after this extremely costly barnstorming trip of ours, we arrived once again at our mountain retreat. I was thinking by this time that we ought to have at least one mountain "advance", but we had lost the battle.

To cap off the catastrophe, only one week after our return, as we were building an addition to the main building, called *Maison Rouge,* a joist-beam fell and landed on my already fully battered skull, resulting in a serious fracture and concussion. This, when added to all the nicks taken in my overworked body by "coincidental accidents" of the years before, was the last note in a symphony of errors!

After the rush to the hospital, during which I passed the time peacefully in my favorite state—a semi-coma—my body was again brought back to the house after it was determined that it was not quite dead enough to bury—but not quite alive enough to walk. They would have kept me in the hospital, but I was discharged and carried out of there by my pupils and taken back home when it was discovered by the hospital staff that I had no medical insurance.

Four and a half months later my consciousness returned somewhat to my almost ruined and pain-wracked body, to my great dismay.

When I first came back to my senses the first thing I discovered was that all those people I had literally paid to remain there by giving them food, clothing, housing, and a personal allowance, in return for which they were to instruct new pupils coming from study groups, with a very few exceptions, as soon as they heard that I might not recover from the accident which had nearly cost me my life, had left for parts unknown.

By the time I could hobble around the house a little, and could go for short walks around the now-empty grounds, I had some idea of the extent of the situation. I could no longer direct the efforts of study group leaders, nor could I even direct the everyday affairs of the Institute. Unless I could get some help, I could not continue in my present condition to give anyone help of any kind.

When my eyesight returned a little, I began to work for a half hour each day on my music and writing, but I was forced to disband all study groups, since most of the group leaders had quit at the news of my accident, and the remaining instructors at the Institute, instead of going to work there with the abandoned groups, left also.

There were a few people still remaining at the Institute and they were able to just barely handle the mail and the daily needs of the building and grounds. I spent most of my remaining energy at that time controlling the outer manifestations of the body so that those hard working staff members who had remained loyal during this crisis would not waste their time worrying over my personal welfare. This was not by any means a noble gesture on my part—there was an enormous amount of work required just to keep the grounds in order, and interference on my behalf would have caused serious problems in maintaining the physical well-being of the Institute.

I began to think seriously about the next steps to be taken since there was at that time a definite chance that I would never again be able to maintain the Institute on the large scale on which it had been operating before my accident. I simply did not have the wherewithal to generate the maintaining impulses for the Institute on a world-wide level as I had earlier.

The time had obviously come for a complete change of plans. I developed, during this quiet time, a set of techniques by which an instructor could give a pupil a daily progressive reading—in map form—of the exact state of his or her essence, and a detailed structural outline—also in map form—of the present state of the psyche. This became useful in the breakdown of the psyche and the eventual dependence on the simple essence for daily life in these pupils of mine still remaining.

At the same time I managed to complete a concrete formulation of the exact method of replacing unconsciously accumulated habits in the essence for consciously created habits which awakened and permanently vivified the essence—on a completely stable basis.

And as I sat in my room upstairs in Maison Rouge, reconstructing my personal method into a form usable by others, and still relatively helpless and bedridden for a large part of each day, even though I was able to get up and walk around for a little while, visitors came to see me and to cheer me up from my despair at seeing the

Institute fall apart, and having my hopes for others collapse with it. And during these visits, I began to notice that even if they came with the most sincere good wishes for my being, and manifested the most positive vibrations possible, I still felt very ill for a long while after they had gone.

I began to wonder about this phenomenon, and soon put my entire intentional thought process to work on it to find out more about it. Finally, after some serious pondering on my part, I realized what was behind the phenomenon. They had all come to wish me well—and the more sincerely they did that, the more they counteracted the effect of my son's efforts to keep my essence alive. In short, while they were within the sphere of my common presence, they became a sort of force-screen which blocked the forces maintaining my essence state, thus allowing my psyche to redevelop itself into its previously powerful self.

I could not possibly allow them to do this to me, and so developed a method by which this would never again occur to me. And this second "little idea" of mine was formulated in the following way:

In the period during which I had made my initial observations of humans, there came to my attention the existence of a survival factor which was aroused whenever the ordinary routine of daily life was in any way threatened or altered for these humans. The trigger which set off this explosive reaction I decided to call a "corn", since it resembled the cause of other explosive reactions resulting from someone accidentally stepping on a growth common to the human foot.

In short, after this experience with well-wishers, whenever anyone came within foot-stomping range, I deliberately and with a hitherto unmatched degree of enthusiasm trod heavily on whichever "corn" was available, arousing inevitably a nearly fatal automatic and uncontrollable rage in everyone connected with me in any way, as a result of having met me or having the slightest good intentions toward me.

And because of the effects of this second little idea of mine, I not only have an assurance of the continued life of my essence, but also I have a continual source of material for my books, since at the moment their corns are trod, the victims of my inexcusably rude behavior immediately and without a second's hesitation whip off their psyches, leaving the raw essence exposed for just a few moments. Of course, in a few cases, when the psyche comes off, there is nothing to take its place at all—no essence. But this is very rare, and the reader should by no means concern himself or herself about it.

Thus I am able to not only maintain my own essence life, but I am also able to determine just how much or how little of their essence has managed to survive the formidable assault of mechanical life on earth, and how much effort will be required—if, indeed, it is still even possible—to remove the degenerative effects of unconscious life among humans. This degenerative effect is one of the reasons that I decided at that point to accept only pupils with a removable psyche. I was forced to concede that those who had not had at least some essence development before the age of twelve had no chance whatever to attain anything—they could no longer change anything in their essences—only the psyche was open to change for them. And so I resolved not to accept anyone as a pupil if they were over twelve years of age—unless accompanied by a child. This was the beginning stage of the nursery and elementary school, toward which all my efforts are now bent.

And this second little idea of mine not only gave me the opportunity to learn about the states of human beings in their essence, but also made it possible for me to experience the loss of not only all material wealth—which had up to then been not inconsiderable—but also many friends and social acquaintances who possessed great material power and could have helped the Institute if I had not stepped on their tender corns—as well as the admiration and envy of many influential beings of the spiritual community, who could no longer lend their support to such an obviously crackbrained idiot as myself. Creating a devil, indeed! And stepping on the corns of poor souls who only wish me the very best! How could I do such things?

And thanks also to the effect produced in the psyches of all unconscious beings by the action of stepping on the afore-mentioned corns, I can be assured that, as long as I continue to manifest such horrible manners, these ideas of mine will never fall into the wrong hands.

FIRST TALK

*Delivered by me to a rather large group of pupils freshly ar-
rived from a gestalt community in northern California on
11 November, 1973*

As you are probably well aware, the projection or inter-
jection of consciousness into the ordinary role-playing of
work, invariably forces one to act out a fantasy in order to
create the assumption that one can be pure essence without
the dissolution of the psyche.

In retroflection, this seems to bring about a self-simulat-
ing mirror in which one's attention can become rooted to
the encounter between one being and another, but the path
of group dynamics in which everyone deeply understands
the group itself, and the growth of one's identity, simply
brings the group into an imaginary reality without really establishing the group consciousness within the eternal contin-
uum.

As the psyche explodes and the essence reaches higher
and higher levels, the explosion is matched and qualified by
a corresponding implosion of identity and awareness. This
results inevitably in the realization of responsibility to other
beings, and particularly toward one's place in the world.

There is a self-initiation which takes place in the primal
scene when objective reality has been attained, perceived,
assimilated, and finally, understood.

There is no compulsion to use computer software in an
effort to control the flow of consciousness, and so there
can be an infinite expansion of the self.

Without defenses, holes in the organism cannot create themselves, and there can be no process taking place. Without a process there can be no identity, for identity itself is only a process, and not an entity.

Integration cannot happen because there is nothing to integrate. The fusion of function and form have at last become an accurate response to the game of life.

The pattern of orientation and non-orientation on which the psyche depends has utterly disintegrated, and the essence is attracted at first exposure to the game of resistance and contact.

Waiting eternally for release from the symbolic the essence becomes both the observer and the object. Feelings and needs are imagined to have an external source, and the factors of reality are disengaged and occluded as attachments to the objects of creation.

The being can no longer remain in the sensation of being focused totally within the unity of the Great Mother.

Self consciousness becomes the background, and otherness becomes the foreground as unfinished perceptual projections appear out there. The inner reality becomes less real than the ongoing external process of the outer world.

The being cannot yet be straight with itself about all this—it must create a cluttered labyrinth of dialogues and presences, of anger, pain and drama, which manipulate it through imaginary outside forces. So the universal con game is continued.

These perception sets in which it sees itself in simulation forces essence into stances of reaction. A distant system, even loaded with elan vital can run away with the being into dream work.

Bad intuition means staying with the game, neither being here, nor being there. The contact-withdrawal game of the primal scene offsets any chance to realize the balance game already happening at the center.

The plastic reality of the highest levels of being combined with fixed ideas and intentions of the psyche to control all this creates an impossibility of awakening into the primal pool with a fully integrated being.

Through the unconscious and automatic tendency to depend upon one's breathing as a cycle-creating and monitoring device, the being has developed within itself incredible tensions and a resistance to letting go when exposed to the flow of reality without a time barrier.

The strength of the universe reflects the power of the being. The material world is a receptacle of concretely formed ideas. The spiritual senses are an interface with which the being is able to monitor the content and context of the universe and give it significance and importance beyond its real meaning-non-meaning.

A confrontation of consciousness with unconsciousness and a refusal to create a bridge between them is an alienation of the interaction between experience and diffusion.

The being's goals are nothing but loose associations of messages on different levels, with the operant model of pathological need for warmth and affection.

Questions are altered and made into verbiage just to maintain the continuity of reaction, response, and doingness.

This split between the conscious essence and the unconscious psyche has caused the being to avoid self simulation at all costs, either by transference or subjectively. Thus it seems to become an individual with individual characteristics and idiosyncrasies, without knowing that it has always had interactive control of any environment.

The effect of this unknowing condition regarding the control of the self and the environment brings about a condition of sadness which is the result of a polarized state of manic hyperactivity and a paranoid interpretation of the desires it is enforcing contrary to its complete lack of desires in the native state.

One is up all the time, continuing to put down creations as a substitute for real self simulation, wearing the masks of beingness and characteristics as a facade.

This self-torture of active and passive outer games takes on its own initiative after a while, leaving the being totally helpless in the grip of its own creations.

A group that remains true to its aim does not become hooked on its own awareness rather than awareness of what is true. In a group the members are continually rehearsing together in preparation for a real confronting, not realizing that this is the real confrontation.

The inner dyad created by the beginning stages of work on oneself is the first indication that something is working inside in the essence. Certain body clues and posture signals tell us that some of the minor fantasies about oneself and the world are beginning to disintegrate.

Expectation and external demands reflect what the individual beliefs are now. Those manifestations which one has inflicted on others and then claimed were manifested by the others begin to fit oneself, and one can finally accept them as his own.

In the second stage of the group game, one tries one's old games out on the group leader, to find out whether one can force the group into theater games with itself.

These blind drawings of projections of one's own games onto a group leader can make the further work of the group if it remains in this state, a great risk.

There is not yet the consideration that each member cannot yet own his own games, and that he or she cannot really tell the other members of the group where he or she had gone to in a moment of disengagement with the universe.

One must finish playing topdog/underdog before one is able to accomplish anything in a group.

In this pretense of being there the real purpose of the group is skillfully avoided. The whole drama of avoidance is the prayer of the psyche that the process become a harmless projection machine in which one can play at encounters in the safe laboratory of the group, where dyads, triads, confrontations and breakthroughs can be experienced without having to be authentic.

A definite signal that the game of avoidance is in progress is the continual use of the phrase "I feel. . ." If in fact there were any real feeling present it would be communicated without words.

The experienced seminarian will prefer the group orgasm in which one can remain silent in the outer world while having one fast game of clever dialogue and smart answers after another.

For the real person even the hottest of hot seat dialogues is not enough. He will demand responsibility for the work, and will refuse the standard psyche which demands admiration, attention, and validation from others.

The real student does not hide out in the gray zone of spontaneously created mental games disguised as emotional uproar.

If a meeting degenerates into the nostalgia of suffering or into a game/non-game of transference of aggressions or passions, the real student will bring it to the zero point because he does not have the time to waste.

Of course everyone in a group will at one time or another have big feelings about everything, and will compulsively act out their prototypic neurosis, but eventually they will learn to put this back where it belongs, in the playpen of the primal pool.

Psychosynthesis forces one to identity in the wrong rhythm. It creates groupies and growthlings—the addicts of self-determinism—who exhibit a continual bald barber syndrome.

Letting it be as it is, and letting go of what you haven't got is getting stuck in the emptiness of the void while trying to hold on to the touchie feelie connection.

One is still masturbating with the self as the imaginary hero of the void.

Simply to learn the language of work and stage it for the ignorant audience is dancing to your own tune. Just at this moment you are the king and queen of tragedy, but we all know that you are playing the game of helplessness and that you have set your own bear traps. So all your complaints that nothing is happening for you is just a pile of elephantshit.

You have been given the method and the idea but not what to do with them, and so the responsibility for getting caught in the hooks of the group game are yours alone.

You no doubt believe firmly by now that nothing less than a giant implosion-explosion will get you out of this.

The mania for receiving grace d-i-r-e-c-t from the Guru is getting to be a regarded form of fantasy about your relationship with the gorilla your dreams and the purpose of his existence as it relates with your own.

It is your own neurotic awareness of space that got you into this self pity process as you wallow in the grief of the lost in space game.

Holding on to the concept of therapy one becomes trapped in the desire for breakthroughs. One can try to allow the fish bowl that is the group process to happen in a real way.

Question: Why do we handle the group process the way we do? Isn't there any way we can learn to be authentic with each other without going into therapeutic trips?

In the psyche there is a never-ending dialogue, a continual round of integration and impasse shuttling back and forth between an inner zone of fantasy, passing through a middle zone of wonder and complexities, and finally through an outer zone of identity and self image.

Thus the anxieties take over and the social programs unfold in an endless flow of delusion, taking on a nightmarish aura of tension and resistance.

The scattered being attempts to center to the psyche, instead of to the essence.

The group leader cannot take responsibility for the way you are. You must decide to own yourself and then develop the will and the means to do it. But before this, study of the current state of the psyche is necessary as a prelude to real work.

Humans believe they are real only because they are out of touch with their primal essence beings.

To exaggerate the toxic effect of the fountain of life is to make contact with the impossible and to be unclear about what it is.

Humans can encounter the Absolute and never notice anything unusual about it.

It is the basic struggle of conscious life versus unconscious life that manipulates the mind and helps it to hide behind growth games and survival games.

You can just watch it or you can become involved in it. One can allow the projection of imaginary reality to create defenses against the real, and instead begin to work on the dream, becoming even more trapped inside the labyrinth.

One may do a round of imaginary reprogramming in a purely sensual impasse of overcoming repressions, and can be there for the dramatization of the depressed state, and yet be completely out of touch with the real by remaining attached to problems and solutions.

These are the results of the masochistic self-torture of the inevitable struggle against ego-boundaries that comes from focusing on the psyche.

Question: How does one begin to do real work on oneself? Is there a specific method we can use?

The method of Self-Study, the observation and cataloging of the contents of the psyche, is not just watching the psyche doing what it does. It is observing the causes of the events that are happening in the here and now. And the causes of the here and now is not something that comes from the past. The causes of the here and now are in the here and now.

One cannot even begin to make real observations unless one knows what to observe, and has at least a taste of who is doing the observing. The essence observes the psyche—and in order to do that, one must quickly learn to feel the difference between the two.

One must begin to make experiments in Self-Study, even if on occasion a mistake is made. It is better in most cases to do it wrong than not to do it at all. A wrong beginning can be corrected, if the psyche does not fight too much against correction, but if no beginning is made, nothing can be corrected, and there is no hope of making any progress from the crystallized psyche state to the open essence state.

Only after a long period of study of the self is it possible to make any correction in the psyche for its eventual dismantling—and only after the psyche is completely gone is it possible to change anything in the essence structure by substituting conscious habits for unconscious ones.

Question: You mentioned earlier the "business of a group. Could you explain a little more about that?

In a formalized study group format the group becomes a regularized expression of the aim to work on oneself, establishing good work habits and providing the tempo for working as a group together.

It is not a pleasant vacation to work in such a group, but a job in which one is working for a boss, even though one has never seen him yet. In order to hold onto the job, one must be productive. Imagine a job in which the boss is always aware of the activities of the worker, and you will understand the situation for yourself.

Question: What if someone comes into a group just to deliberately or compulsively disrupt the group work?

If a power struggle for domination of the group occurs, the group should be disbanded and re-established under a different and more experienced group leader if possible.

If this cannot be accomplished, then the group must disperse and reestablish itself under different conditions, if indeed any further work is possible for members of that group.

However, within any group organized along any lines, there is always a certain amount of bullshit going on. You will inevitably see that some members of the group are in the group just to act out their identities and beliefs.

Eventually most of the individuals in the group will cut through the desire trip and go for the game beyond the game. The others who hang back can be left behind in the study group, and the ones who break through the influence and power games can be passed on to a work group.

Question: *Should we try to stop ourselves from manifesting bad habits if we observe them in ourselves during Self-Study?*

You should never change what you are using for Self-Study. What will you have left if all that is gone? You may not like what you see in yourself once you begin to look at it, but you should be able to realize that none of that is yours anyway—it all comes from conditioning and programming. If you feel guilty or ashamed about having those things in there, you are identifying with the psyche, and not with the essence.

When you try to make contact with the essence, and you bring that part of the essence into the psyche, or into the mentally controlled part of yourself, you remove one more possible means of contact with the essence. Leave the hook in the fish's mouth until you can pull it into the boat.

Through observation and Self-Study you will see many things to which you are clinging, and you will have the automatic desire to free yourself from them before you are ready. If you do somehow manage to release them, you will only take other things in their place, because they cannot be eliminated, just replaced. These new things may be more invisible to you, making it much worse than before. It is better to have something there that you know about than something you cannot see at all.

Question: When does all this game playing stop?

Psychosis has its limitations. To repeat your lying as if it were truth and to play the game of group catastrophe will eventually result in the rest of the group becoming outraged at the waste of their time, and they will stop it themselves.

Even if a group went on a total binge of workshop marathons nothing would happen in a real way as long as one or two people take up the group's time in personal psyche games. Eventually everyone in the group will realize this and take steps to stop it or to remove the person blocking the group's aim to do real work.

Question: If we give up the psyche, does that mean that we will lose our individuality and spontaneity?

The essence is very simple. It is composed of only eighteen very basic habits. Habits are automatic thoughts and actions which are really forms of identity. So the essence thinks in pure basic identities, and acts in completely automatic sequences based on a preset scenario. There are nine possible identities the essence can manifest, and nine possible scenarios. It makes one seem very dull or boring to others who are complicated—or seem complicated—because they have an unimaginable number of temporary identities and scenarios supplied by the psyche, which collects these from social conditioning and fantasies of the mind.

SECOND TALK

Delivered by me on July 17th, 1973 in Montreal to a group of about one hundred and fifty persons who were members of a study group formed six months earlier

I have been pondering the question which has arisen for your group. You have told me that as a group you often express things outwardly that you do not genuinely feel in your inner world reality. That is the same thing as saying that you are insincere.

You obviously need some help with this problem, but it is only a symptom of a much deeper problem that you have not yet become aware of. I am going to call this deeper problem to your attention now—but according to all that I have found out about you in the past few days, you are not able to digest anything whole. So I am not only going to cut this data up into small pieces, but I am boiling it and putting it into the blender in order to thoroughly liquify and predigest it for you, also putting in the necessary transforming factors corresponding to enzymes, spices, and factors for the arousal and preservation of "friendly intestinal flora".

My great aim in allowing the formation of study groups was to create a definite division of work and focusing points in the school, so that people would be able to work at their own pace and open up to a pure essence state in small easy stages.

In this system of division, there are three main groups— an outer school, a middle school, and an inner school.

In the outer school, composed of study groups and public talks and demonstrations, would be those pupils who have just recently discovered the possibility of work and who require a foundation for understanding the work and the direction of work on oneself.

In the middle school, composed of work groups, would be those pupils who have earned the right to work in a practical way on those ideas which they have up to that time been only studying and applying to themselves on a small scale.

In the inner school the pupils become instructors and learn to pass on to others what they have learned to apply in themselves.

Now that I have provided for you a more or less plain and maybe oversimplified sketch of the format of the school, I want to describe to you one of the most basic forms of study vital to the dissolution of the outer self, the psyche, and the substitution of the inner self, the essence.

This program of work in which we study the psyche in order to learn enough about it to dismantle it is called Self-Study. The whole of self study is composed of observation of the self. What is it we are calling the self? Is it the inner being? The real you? No, it is the entire collection of social conditioning, mental programs, and beliefs held by the mind. This is called the psyche. It includes the sense of identity created by the perception of the whole of this mash-mosh of patterned behavior and thought.

How is Self-Study done? At first one observes only the physical manifestations of the body—the facial expressions, the postures, the communication signals of the physical form. One sees the things that one does with the body and facial expression just to get along all right and make others feel comfortable about one.

Next, one observes—but does not try to change—those expressions of insincerity which one makes automatically and verbally to others, which one feels one must make in order to get along with others. Here we see the things we feel we must say and do so that others will not harm us, and so they will accept us. These are the social machinery forced upon one by the culture, but which are not part of the ordinary functions of the machine called the human body. They are artificial impulses placed there to make one become part of the human race as it currently understands itself and its world.

One can observe in this way the unbelievable amount of insincerity required of one just to function and to earn a livelihood in this enlightened atomic age society.

Finally, when life no longer holds any promises for one, and there is no need for anything the world has to offer in a material way, one can begin to eliminate the psyche and expose the essence in a stable and permanent state, thus earning for oneself the title and reputation of a fool.

During the past two years at the Institute when only the exoteric studies were able to be introduced, thanks to the accident I have frequently mentioned which fractured my skull and left me bedridden for four months, people came through the school thinking that they had been given the whole teaching on all three levels, without any preparation on their part, and that they had suddenly without any effort toward it, become "conscious", which is the usual definition of someone who has destroyed the psyche and is existing in a pure essence state. I might add that even after this is accomplished it takes many years to alter the essence from an accumulation of unconscious habits to a formation of conscious habits. They had done all this in a matter of weeks or several months of work—mostly reading and discussion—and were now on their way to become teachers, since I was safely out of the way. They did not count on my survival, however, and now that I am able to call their game, we will see some sparks fly.

After the Institute emptied like a sinking ship, these unfortunate victims of tunnel vision using only the most fragmentary elements of the teaching, began to personally profit from these ideas in order to be able to live on the scale to which they would like to have become accustomed, but this time instead of taking as pay for passing these ideas on to others something for their essence, they decided to take money for the use of their non-existent psyches.

And if not for these slim gleanings taken from the exoteric studies, they would have been forced to live according to their real beings, on an ordinary level of existence.

But in all these cases of the unconscious and mechanical presentation of what they thought was the teaching, only one or two aspects of the teaching were focused upon as if they had been the entire teaching.

In short, they presented only those ideas in which they were personally interested, and ignored other parts of the teaching which they did not like or agree with, or which violated their already crystallized beliefs.

In fact, if they had not told their students that they were conscious, the students might have thought that they still functioned according to the psyche and ordinary habits of a human being, with the usual tendencies of aggressions, passions, negative emotions, and desires of an ordinary human being who has never done a shred of work on himself or herself.

But in addition to the presence in them of the ordinary forms of consciousness containing fear, envy, hatred, anger, vanity and jealousy, there also exists in them the formation of a peculiar function of the psyche—that of only taking in data in a superficial way and giving it back in pieces without regard to the present situation.

In short, they were able to remember a few things they had heard or read but did not form in themselves any real use for it, and so give it out to others more or less in a hodge-podge fashion, not according to need.

But even if only in possession of bits and pieces of the full teaching, they assume that they received all of it, and that thinking and reading about it is as good as learning to apply it. To this day they refuse to hear that they only received a small portion of it, and that if not for themselves at least for the sake of their students they are welcome to come back and receive the rest of it, in spite of everything they have done since they decided to personally profit from the teaching, they simply say in that tone only becoming to a cornered fox, "You just want me to come back so that you can take advantage of me again."

It is interesting to note that these purveyors of ancient wisdom and compassionate knowledge who had been fed, clothed, and cared for in every possible way by my efforts, were not in the least interested in my welfare when they left the Institute—some within hours after the accident was announced to the students. And they are afraid I am going to take advantage of them again!

No, I would not do the same thing twice, having already made a gross error in dealing with humans. Now they will have to pay at least a thousand dollars a month to stay at the Institute, just so they do not complain again about this.

According to the period in which these teachers attended the Institute, they each were exposed to a different aspect of the teaching. Had they remained for the length of time recommended by me as the minimum period required for the full presentation of the teaching, and then gone into the middle and inner schools for the assimilation of what they had learned, they would today be able to apply consciously the whole of the method, and not simply throw fragments of it around at random.

But they felt the need to leave in order to get something for their psyches in the outer world, before they had received anything real, beyond simply information. And so they remembered only those parts of the teaching which reinforced their beliefs, needs, and urges.

One of these teachers began a school which has as its

central—and only—belief the idea that man is composed
of three separate bodies and brains, all acting independently, and that if this is understood even only intellectual-
ly, the being will develop into a real soul.

This was of course only a way of explaining the function of the psyche, and had nothing whatever to do with
the essence.

Another teacher coming out of this exoteric tradition,
who incidentally only lasted several weeks and whom I
cannot recall having ever met personally, is presently
teaching—supposedly with my consent—that my entire
system is based on suffering, which is required in order
to form the soul, and that pulling out the toenails with
pliers is the only method that works. He never heard or
saw this at the Institute, and in fact was asked to leave
when he performed this grisly ritual in front of his study
group one evening.

Another of these conscious teachers believes that a
compression of time and events is the only way to en-
lightenment, and that everyone must learn to do this.
So he started a school in which everyone sits opposite
each other for a weekend and asks the question "Who
are you?"

Still another firmly believes that so long as an action is
intentional—regardless of other factors of conscience, compassion, and hospitality—then it must also be "conscious",
or that is to say, "from essence". And so he began the
*Intentional Masturbation And Salt-Dropping School Of
Conscious Actions"* in New York and Northern California,
of course charging a pretty penny to those who wish to further crystallize—and perhaps even to make immortal—those
precious psyches of theirs, thus insuring that the Work will
never disturb them in the future as it has in the past.

Yet another completely believes—according to her own
quite urgent "needs below the abdomen"—that the sexual
fluids used to form a new child are the real means for perfecting oneself and that no other factors have any importance whatever in the formation of the higher bodies. It is
of course useless to reason with biology.

Another of these teachers is completely convinced that
Self-Study is the only solution to the problems of life. He
found that this little idea could be used to excuse the most
outrageous and stupid conduct imaginable by saying "It's
all right, I'm observing my self do it."

And those interested in mathematics and music liked
the idea that the essence and the psyche are constructed
of double helix formations in octaves of nine each, total-
ling eighteen possible combination forms.

Then those who received the idea of creating an external
devil and then exiling it forever into the outer darkness have
managed to make a religion out of that. Then there are the
former pupils who believe that just through the repetition
of the phrase "I Am" they will become conscious. They
have each taken a Sunday discussion and blown it up out of
all proportion.

These people have such a high idea of themselves that
they cannot even be told that they were never admitted to
the middle school, let alone the inner school!

They have become such true believers in their own infal-
libility and knowledge that they cannot believe that they
were never given more than just a light introduction to the
ideas.

Their psyches have become so crystallized that they are
not now able to work. Their fears have become so real for
them that the specter of deep searching work still before
them looms so dreadful that they will never be able to overcome it unless something spectacular happens for them.

And that is why I have decided to reorganize the Institute
along completely new lines. . . in which you will be invited
to take only a fringe part.

I have decided to take as pupils only those who have at
least some chance. So far no one who has had no work in
the early years of their lives has gone even one millionth
of the way toward essence-life, and this has been discour-
aging to say the least.

It is possible for some people to dismantle the psyche,
but only if they have been able to retain a plastic personality, which occurs only in those who have had some work

in childhood.

This means that I will not accept anyone for work at
the Institute who is over the age of twelve. Any parents
who wish to participate as day helpers or staff volunteers
must be accompanied by a child.

I intend to provide a training program—unobtrusively
couched in play, of course—in which the child is taught
to imitate the forms of social conditioning and behavior
limits without having to form a psyche in order to have
knowledge, relationship skills, communication skills, and
mechanical and business abilities. Thus they will be able
to remain in essence and still seem human to others.

Work on social drama and instantaneous learning techniques will be offered, but not enforced. Even so, experimental work with my own children and other children at
the Institute in the past has shown that without enforce-
ment the children are willing to accept social limits quite
cheerfully as if real, if they know that these limits are de-
manded by society but do not have to seem real to them
in their inner lives. Of course they do not talk about this
in such technical language, but they can do it. It has always been a source of laughter for me to see that those
who can discuss it can't do it, and those who can do it
don't discuss it. All this is by the way of making you,
the parents of potential students, comfortable about it.

In a way it is too bad that no one in your generation
will be able to go very far, with the exception of a few
who dropped out in disgust, having never accepted the
formation of the human psyche in the first place. But
they have already found the work, and were in it for a
long time before you even knew it existed. Now you are
interested, but for you it is too late. You can serve, however, as boosters for the next generation. With your help,
even though you cannot now succeed, they may be able
to.

There will of course be some training for the parents, but only insofar as is necessary to make certain that the parents do not interfere with or counter the efforts made for the children in the school. I should warn you now that you will be required to live the rest of your life—as long as the children are with you—without ever manifesting a negative emotion either in front of them or when they are away or in another room.

In the Method, the child learns to imitate the forms and abilities of the psyche, and to instantaneously create, change, or cease creating, any personality at will. Since the child will only do this with those who require a psyche to relate with, the child may at first frighten you by not having any personality at all. It will be like living with a zen master who seems to be too small to be so old. But the need for relating through the psyche may be in you, too, and the child will eventually learn that it is not safe to relate to you in essence, if you demand it.

I can understand why you might resent the child's lack of a psyche, and his or her permanent essence state, but after a while you will get used to it.

As for you in this group, you are still welcome to take the Practitioner's Course, the SixWorld Intensives, and other such activities we will offer to adults on the basis that one should never give up hope, even when there is none.

. . . And of course there is always Supergame.

supergame
465-4098

Supergame business card 1968

MAN'S INNER AND OUTER LIFE: PSYCHE & ESSENCE

*The following dialogue occurred as a demonstration of the
ordinary function of the psyche in translating from outer
world to essence, and from essence to outer world. We can
see the alteration of information as it passes through the
psyche.*

Today we are going to have what is called "Darshan".
In this special Darshan, not like other forms of Darshan,
you will be able to observe the translating action of the
psyche as it passes data to and from the essence into the
outer world and from it.
  Bob, here, will act as the psyche, filtering information
as it comes from the essence, and filtering it again as it
comes from the outer world to the essence.

G. *Okay, Bob—find out if anyone here has any money.
    And watch your language when you talk to Ameri-
    cans—they're very sentimental about money.*
B. I will translate into english for Baba. He says that
    he wishes to welcome you Americans to our coun-
    try, and that even though we are very poor, we ex-
    tend our hospitality, humble though it may be, to
    all of you.
S. *Baba, I don't know what to do in order to become
    conscious.*
G. *Give that student some candy—maybe he'll shut up.*
B. Baba says: consciousness can sometimes be transmit-
    ted through objects or food. Even candy can con-
    tain shaktipat.

G.   *Some of these candies are chocolate filled, and some
     of them are caramel. Hard to tell with this damn
     milk chocolate covering. I might have to eat every
     one of these things to find one soft one.*

B.   Baba says: One must always search for the inner
     nature of everything, and in order to do this, one
     must sample all of life.

S.   *Baba, I bring flowers as an offering.*

G.   *What is this, the Rose Parade? Put those flowers
     with the rest of them. (to the student who has ap-
     proached with the bouquet) Flower killer!*

B.   Baba says: A gift of beauty such as this will not go
     unnoticed in the world to come.

S.   *Baba, if no soul can be lost, then why should I work
     to develop? Won't I be able to just sit back and wait
     for the inevitable?*

G.   *What'd he say?*

B.   He said he wants to goof off for another fifty billion
     years.

G.   *Maybe you had better find out the difference between
     "recognition of something real within you" and "wish-
     ful thinking", good buddy.*

B.   Baba says: You are very wise, and he is sure you are
     correct about this. If one waits long enough, the inevi-
     table will eventually occur.

S.   *Oh, Baba, I'm so happy to be here with you!*

G.   *What'd she say?*

B.   She says she likes the atmosphere.

S.   *I have always wanted to come here to your country
     in order to study the science of the soul, Baba.*

G.   *What?*

B.   I told you. She said she likes the atmosphere.

G.   *Oh. (to the student) You ever been to this country be-
     fore?*

B.   (to the student) Have you visited our country before?

S.   *Not in this lifetime, but I think I was incarnated here
     as a Brahmin or a Saint. I'm trying to clear up the de-
     tails in my morning meditation.*

G.   *What'd she say, Bob?*

B.   She said "No".

G.   *Well, tell her something and get the next one up here.*

B.   Baba says: It is good that you have come here again to taste the fruits of your previous incarnations in this land which has always cultivated the spiritual life.

S.   *Baba said all that in those few words he spoke?*

G.   *What's she saying?*

B.   She wants to know if you said all that in just a few words.

G.   *Tell her to screw.*

B.   Baba says: Yes. It takes but a few words in our native language to express these ideas, while in english the language was not developed to express spiritual ideas so it takes more words.

G.   *Here, take this candy.*

B.   (to the student) Here, take this candy.

S.   *I'd rather not. . .My teeth get cavities rather easily.*

G.   *What?*

B.   She says she's cavity-prone.

G.   *You better take this candy, or I'll bust you in the snout.*

B.   Baba says: The Guru is not fooling. Eat the candy. *(another student comes up to the stage)*

S.   *This is for you, Baba.*

G.   *What's this stuff?*

B.   Baba wishes to know what it is that you have brought.

S.   *This is a homemade cheese, organically produced without rennets. It comes from goat's milk—raw—and I make it according to an old recipe from a commune I once lived at. It's completely pure and I made sure my vibes were good all the time I worked on it. If I felt bad or had my period I didn't even go into the same room with it. I hope Baba likes it.*

B.   She says it's some cheese.

G.   *What does she want? Why'd she come here, anyway?*

B. Baba wishes to know why you seek this knowledge.

S. *What knowledge? I just came here to bring him this cheese, that's all.*

G. *What'd she say?*

B. She says she doesn't know why she's here.

G. *Of course she doesn't know! If she knew, she would be someplace else! That's why she's here!*

B. Baba says to thank you for your effort to bring him this wonderful homemade cheese.
    (another student approaches)

G. *Ah, another sucker.*

S. *What did Baba say?*

B. He said: Approach me, seeker, and receive my blessing.

S. *Baba, I have come all the way from America to be with you. I hitchhiked across three continents just to be here. Please accept me as a student, and let me kiss the dust on your feet.*

G. *What?*

B. He says he didn't bring any money with him.

S. *Baba, although I have nothing material to offer you for your work, I brought some flowers.*

G. *What kind of flowers are those, petunias?*

B. Baba wishes to know what kind of flowers they are.

S. *These are carnations, Baba.*

G. *What?*

B. He says those are petunias.

G. *That's what I thought they were.*
    (another student approaches)

S. *Baba, please give me some advice about my meditation. I keep having negative thoughts.*

G. *What?*

B. He wants to know what to think about.

G. *Tell him something wise and get him out of here.*

B. Baba says: To the sweet man, sick tastes bitter.

(another student approaches)

S. *Baba, what is the meaning of human life on earth?*

G. *What did he want?*

B. He asked the usual question.

G. *Well, give him the usual answer.*

B. Baba says: Each must seek, and each must answer.

S. *Baba, I have brought you this check for fifty thousand dollars.*

G. *Whoops—you don't have to translate that one. How far can we get on fifty grand?*

B. This present is like water to the soul, and Baba will be able to put it to good use immediately.

G. *Okay, you keep it going, while I duck out of here and put a hold on this at the bank.*

B. What'll I tell them?

G. *Say something wise. . .chant. . .anything. I'll be back as soon as I can.*

B. Baba will return in a moment. He said to explain some of the finer points of philosophy to you in the meantime. . . A dream is only the wish of the soul to awaken. . . The spirit is like the wind, never resisting, without beginning and without end, not to be broken, but only bent. . . Little ideas begin in the mind, but real thoughts begin in the soul. . . A spirit is like a grape on the vine—it can become wine or food for the scavenger, and he who wishes to produce wine with it must preserve it and nourish it. . . Meditation is the home of the spirit and the stillness of the mind. . . A bird in the hand is worth two in the bush. . . A penny saved is a penny earned. . . A stitch in time saves nine. . . Give 'em an inch and they take a mile. . . Mary, Mary, quite contrary, how does your garden grow? . . Uh, uh, Needle in a haystack. . .uh, uh, A fool and his money are soon—hey, you're back already!

G. *Yeah, the check cleared. Let's get out of here.*

B. Lucky you showed up when you did. I was running out of wise sayings. (to the group) Baba says thank you all for coming to Darshan, and good afternoon.

G. (To the group)
This little drama of ours today represents man's ordinary condition, and how the psyche translates and filters what the essence sends out and receives back. This is not a representation of an essence being, but an ordinary man. The inner world has become entirely dominated by the psyche, and the psyche makes everything all right for everyone, wishing to offend no one, and to be liked and admired by everyone. What a mess!

EXERCISES FOR CONSCIOUS LIFE

In this next to last chapter I intend to give you a few
simple hints of some things you can do in order to get at
least a good look at the psyche, and perhaps change a few
of its habits—easier than changing the essence-habits, and
good practice. I do this once again with that well-wishing
hope of mine, to hope where there is no hope.

1.   *Prayer Hands*
At the very first moment of awakening in the morning,
fold the hands into a prayer position, palm to palm. Try
to remember to do this, and make it the first thought
you have in the morning.

2.   *Die At Night*
As you drift off to sleep, get the idea that if you fall asleep, you will die.

3.   *Morning Gratitude*
Upon awakening in the morning, feel gratitude that you
woke up this morning, and that you have at least one
more day of life in which to try to dismantle the psyche
before you die and it is ripped off you explosively.

4.   *Word Invention*
Every day invent a word that you have never heard before. Invent a definition for it, too, and record it in
your diary.

5.   *Categories*
Every day, point out five different objects to yourself,
and ask yourself "What is that object?" and "What is its
use?" Invent a completely non-human answer, an answer that does not depend upon psychological or physical explanations.

6.   *Self-Study*
Observe those moments of insincerity when the psyche
takes over or maintains control. Watch for moments in
which stress forces the psyche to drop away for a while,
and see what the essence does, what habits it is compos-
ed of, and how well it is suited to conscious life. Each
evening record a list of your insincerities:
Do you smile too much?
Talk too much?
Explain too much?
Are you sympathetic when you aren't even interested?
Do you try to make others feel better about things?
Do you laugh at jokes and stories that are not funny?

7.   *Time Bridge*
Each evening decide upon a specific useless but harmless action to be carried out at a specific time the next
day. Record the intended action in your diary. The
following day, record the results.

8.   *Itch Exercise*
When an itch develops and you become aware of it, do
not scratch it. Pay attention to it, and allow awareness
of it to grow in your consciousness. Finally, only after
you are certain that you have overcome the urge to
scratch, go ahead and scratch it.

9.   *Change of Habit*
Find in yourself a harmless, useless, and insignificant
habit—not an automatic thing, like a tic—and change it.
If you normally scratch your nose with your left hand,
use the right instead. Little habits only, nothing dangerous or powerful. Someday maybe you will be able
to change one of your essence habits—one of the immortal ones that create your karma.

10.   *New Thing*
Each day do something—at least one thing, no matter
how small—that you have never done before.

Now I will outline some group exercises to be done in a Study Group. I will just name them and describe them in a short blurb, because these need to be demonstrated by a coach, and then the coach needs to correct them from day to day or from week to week, depending upon how often the group meets. These were not intended to be performed by oneself, but within a group context.

G1   *Hand Exercise*
Sit at a table. Hold your arm bent upward from the elbow, fingers extended, palm toward the face, about one foot away. Look at the hand until it becomes for you a being with its own will, essence, and mind. Then have it return to its everyday state.

G2   *Gym*
Every day, do the stress exercises for breaking down the psyche. The psyche closes down under stress. Go far beyond your limit, but allow the coach to hold you back if you push the organism too far.

G3   *Breathing*
Your coach will help you discover the correct breathing pattern for the Gym, so that you do not alter the organism radically during the physical exercises.

G4   *Idiot Exercises*
The coach will have you perform various personality types and plastic masks of psyches different than your own.

G5   *Readings*
The instructor or group leader will give you a weekly reading, showing you in map-style the exact contents of your essence, and the exact contents of your psyche, and which habit is dominant at that time.

G6   *Group Exercises*
These are performed by the entire group. A tape recording has been made of one such group exercise, called **The Limits Game**. (note: this tape is available from Iman Tape Service)

G7   *History*
Each day write one chapter of personal history of how you came into the work, and what has happened to you as a result since then.

Many of the pupils—and not a few journalists—have asked what the basis for this teaching is and where it came from. In an unusually candid moment such as this, I feel it is time to unmask at least some of the origin of my work in its present form.

Back in the mid-fifties there was formed a group of individuals who each had a "specialty", but in spite of this knowledge found that it was no use by itself. And so a small and serious group of specialists banded together under the name *The Fellowship of the Ancient Mind*, which group I have at various times called "Sneakers After Truth" and "The Goon Squad".

Each of us had, as I have already mentioned, some small fragment of knowledge. Ron M. had a knowledge of hypnosis but no understanding of why it worked. Michael S. had a working knowledge of the Corridor of Madness—and in fact having long ago made his more or less permanent home there had been functioning as a guide for others who found themselves trapped there or just passing through.

Roger and Diane B. brought their specialty of psychic phenomena. They were able to arouse very spectacular effects—but also were unable to control them or explain them to their satisfaction.

Jim P. was a specialist in architecture, and had learned to read the books hidden in medieval cathedrals and saints' shrines or tombs.

James S. was a specialist in the manufacture of ritual objects, and could create an atmosphere which would instantly cause specific and similar reactions in everyone who came into these spaces.

Glenn H. was a specialist in ceremonial magic and in particular the works of Kelly, the Bavarian Illuminati, the Golden Dawn and MacGregor Mathers, the O.T.O. and Aleister Crowley, the black magician who scandalized Europe and the United States in the mid-twenties.

Trulee F. was an archaeologist and Egyptologist. She had already several years before joining the Fellowship managed to decode many of the ancient temple and burial ritual dances and had developed a shorthand notation for choreography of dances similar to those used in mime and ballet.

Hassan was an expert in Persian, Turkish, Armenian, and Tibetan, and served as chief cook on our journeys. He was familiar with the knowledge of "transforming factors" in food—spices and herbs which made food a new substance which could utilize the results of breath and impressions for material for the development of the essence. He had also studied with the Mevlevi in Konya, Turkey, and been the personal secretary for the founder of a great world religion in Indonesia for some years.

Michael Valentine wandered into the Fellowship meeting room directly off a ship from New Zealand and announced that he had no idea what he was doing there, but had felt the urgent call to walk along this street and come into this building and this office. He was an expert in the understanding of martial arts and their origin.

Jerry E. was an old carnival barker and bally man. His father had been the owner of a midget act in the Barnum and Bailey circus. He brought with him an uncanny ability to "read" someone's psychology even before talking with him—especially that of a potential "mark".

Randy was a member of the Magic Castle and of the Society of American Magicians, and brought to our group the ability to see and understand the techniques of fake phenomena, especially mental and spiritist tricks, so that we could recognize real phenomena when we saw it, and knew how to test those things we experienced.

Father Michael I. brought to the group the knowledge of the church ritual and catechism, the method of preserving knowledge in religious forms. He also brought with him the understanding of the work of Gomidas, who had created a perfect replica of the Angelic Host in his music and cathedral staging.

There was a *dvoorak,* who told stories that had been passed on from generation to generation without change, and had been given simple wisdom that only a real fool can see. He brought to the group the ability to be a fool without being a stupid fool. He also brought ancient wisdom in a form which could be decoded if we knew the language and method of encoding. In this endeavor Trullee and Hassan proved to be the primary agents. To this true wise fool we owed all our information on hidden brotherhoods and the means to find them again in modern times.

There were others who wish to remain anonymous even to the extent that their names not be changed, and in respect to this wish of theirs I have not mentioned them or the specialty which they brought to the group. However, every one of these specialties became necessary for the discovery of the location of the hidden brotherhoods in which we were able to receive the means to crystallize our separate knowledge into a unified and coherent whole, and it is thanks to all these people in the Fellowship, both those who actually went on the expeditions and those who backed them financially or who provided clues by sharing their branch of knowledge, that this and other schools exist today.

The first expedition resulting from data extracted from the temple dances of Egypt, Thailand, Cambodia and Bali—along with certain rituals observed by the inhabitants of Bali in which sounds are used for the balance of the organism—which said ritual is called "Ketchjak"—led to the establishment of a permanent center for the logging and assimilation of data coming directly through theatrical methods of transmission from ages past, and to the second and more important mission from the standpoint of forseeable results, in which a dozen of the Fellowship traveled through the Ethiopian mountains in search of a secret method of movements training called "Wud-Sha-Lo" which could be used as a system of movement, or as a system of self-defence, or as a book in which specific techniques of separating psyche and essence and substituting unconscious habits in the essence with conscious habits which constrained one to automatically live a conscious life, and techniques for bringing an individual to the door of the Corridor of Madness and for fusing the ordinary centers of function—the thinking, feeling, and automatic and moving centers—into a single unified being. Not only this, but within the system of movement it was said to contain the Method for fusing, perfecting and crystallizing all seven bodies possible for humans on earth.

In this expedition, two members of the party were killed, one died of poisoning from the bad food, or from some sort of bacterial infection, and three others left in the middle of the effort. Of the remaining members, only three have put into practice what was learned from this transmission from the ancient world. All the others have either gone on as before, which is to say in the same old way before they joined the Fellowship, without synthesizing and assimilating what they had learned, or have "returned to the ordinary life", or have gone into seclusion in monasteries or within some of the secret brotherhoods discovered in various expeditions. One of the members of the Fellowship has been adopted into the Apache tribe and is now accepted as a Shaman. It was this individual, Steve M., who brought to the group the idea of a modern technical manual outlining the procedures and methods for preventing the reconstitution of the psyche in the Corridor of Madness.

Yet another member who wishes to remain silent and anonymous, yet who is offering the results of our researches to some pupils coming from ordinary life, contributed the concept of the Corridor of Madness itself—that point and period in which the psyche breaks down, exposing the pure essence, and during which the psyche rebuilds or is "reborn" unless one knows how to keep the psyche from reforming, and has mastered the method of "remaining in essence" or "in the void of the Clear Light".

During this period we learned how to form study groups and how to transmit knowledge—and build a bridge to understanding—for others. This is no secret. Yet very few will actually use and apply this knowledge. That is the secret.

The members of a study group are like mountain climbers in many ways. At first, they have only heard about the view from the peak, but although they wish to see it also, nobody wants to make the effort to climb the mountain. They come up with plans for flying a helicopter up there and landing it on the summit, or buying a picture of it from someone who has been there.

They would prefer that someone chop the tip of the mountain off and bring it down to them. But this does not show them the view. Sooner or later they realize that they are going to have to make the climb themselves, and they begin to do it.

Then, during the climb, some of them will get tired and want the others to carry them. But again this is not possible, because everyone needs all the energy they have for their own climb upward. There is none to spare for carrying another—although there is enough to spare for helping one another. But help does not mean to do for someone else. It means to help someone overcome the inner obstacles—and in some cases, the outer obstacles—preventing one from doing for oneself.

In a group, just as in mountain climbing, everyone is attached for safety to everyone else. If one falls, the others can just lift him up again by the rope. If they allow one to fall and do not lift him up, they all eventually fall with him.

If one makes it to the summit, then the entire group makes it to the summit, because the first one there can pull the others up by the safety cable. Only if everyone in the group gets to the summit will the group succeed in its aim. No one individual out of the group can attain it on his own, since he is attached by rope to the others.

It is a very important thing that every member of the group attend every single meeting. There is nothing that is more important in life for real mountain climbers. If one member consistently fails to show up, he or she is cut away from the safety cable and sent down the mountain, because the group's aim is endangered by a dilettante.

As you work you will find that your desire for conscious life, real essence life, will grow stronger. You may not even be able to sleep at night from time to time, because this desire will grow on you. You may eventually seem to "froth at the bit", until nothing but the attainment of conscious life has any meaning for you. That is almost powerful enough as an aim to keep you going far enough to succeed. To this must be added a persistent "itch" that cannot be scratched by anything short of essence life and the complete dismantling of the psyche.

The group should take complete precedence in your life. It must be more important even than a Saturday night date. Before one can enter a work group, the aim must be tested. One of the tests is regular attendance in a study group for a long period of time.

In a study group some exercises are introduced. After a while in the study group, more advanced techniques will be given. In the beginning, many demands are made, and very few explanations are given. Later, explanations will be offered.

In regard to continued membership in the group, nothing is certain. If a member is not productive to the group aim, he or she will have to leave the group. Those who are argumentative, or who have come only to find a forum for their own beliefs or problems of the psyche are eliminated from the group.

Only those who belong in such a group are permitted to remain. This does not mean that only "yes-men", "ass-kissers" and "zombies" are allowed in a group. It means that only those who wish to work hard to make this kind of effort, and who genuinely wish for themselves a pure essence life are permitted in the group. For those who wish a discussion group in order to debate philosophy, such a group would be a waste of time, in any case.

Unless they become necessary for the group, new ideas will not be introduced just to make it interesting. Thus meetings may not be very exciting for the psyche. But perhaps you can taste the real feeling of conscious life already.

APHORISMS

1. *The self must learn to love life in order to appreciate death before death.*

2. *To become conscious is to see the world in essence at all times.*

3. *To throw the psyche off the shoulders—to relieve oneself of the burden at last—this is the real meaning of the phrase "to enlighten".*

4. *Acceptance of one's real nature—the habit to be— requires continual practice at being this nature until it forms permanently within oneself.*

5. *The disintegration of ordinary perception in favor of direct perception is the chemistry of symbolic reality exploding inside the psyche.*

6. *The impulse of self-preservation is the last struggle of the psyche against the essence.*

7. *The Here and Now reality does not require any action from you.*

8. *Your presence is a powerful enough assumption to actively prevent completion of the self.*

9. *The path made by the guides is the way of recognit-ion within yourself.*

10. *The Holy and Sacred action of worship sustains the application of work disciplines. One must never for-get that behind it all lurks the powerful action of God.*

11. *To recognize God in the action of self-perfection is to trust in the common ground of the teaching.*

12. *Remaining true to one's vows is the most important of all actions of the conscience.*

13. *The lost and found of the being is the invasion of the vessel by the Holy Ghost.*

14. *The church level of past beliefs cannot now fulfill the Yoga of Grabbing The Tail Of The Tiger.*

15. *The path of separate rehabilitation perpetuates the myth of the teacher-student story.*

16. *The transformation of the human being to an essence being is the result of the individual to direct the divine impulses of eternity.*

17. *In the game of destruction of the ego, the winning and losing atmosphere of the achiever can be dis-pensed with.*

18. *The anger and grief of self-pity creates the apathy of self-love.*

19. *The communion of the self is the prayer of the image to the certainty of the void.*

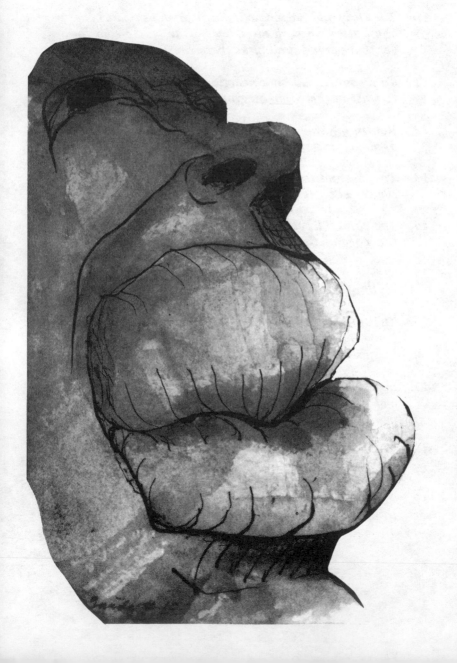

20. *Opening the soul to growth is the myth of truth.*

21. *The ignorance and arrogance of the psyche reality is a fake but convincing system.*

22. *The inconvenience of real work makes the treatment of the personality a good game.*

23. *The pain of joy and the joy of pain ignores the real nature of the Clear Light Reality, and at the moment of recognition substitutes the Christ for the gorilla.*

24. *The seeker-priest is the way in the work when with inner understanding the hidden becomes known.*

25. *The perfected man is the dervish devil-saint formed by the contemplation of the divine birth and the wish for the formation of the soul.*

26. *The question of common sense in the joyous journey is the psalm of the cycle of the repetitive, the offspring of the effect of sacred food, the doxology of the secular.*

27. *Grounding the laws of three, seven, and nine, is the door to the Rose Garden—the unity of the essence with the outer form.*

28. *The circular path of the seeker is the mystical fool in the Temple of Samsara.*

29. *The blessing of the Grace of the Light opens the heart to prayer in the Ministry of Sacrifice.*

30. *The liberation of awareness is the chant of the earth.*

48) GUIDE No. 6, 1975   5"x7"

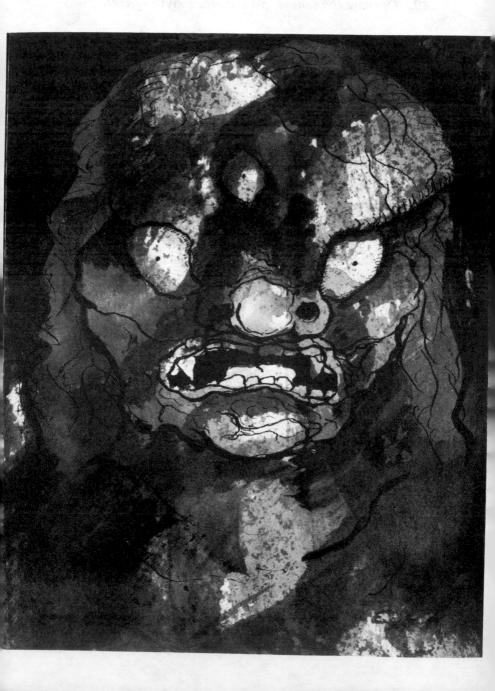

31. *The essence being is a familiar friend to the space of the cosmic joke.*

32. *The centered diamond body is the sacred cow of the bell, book, and candle—the bible of reality.*

33. *The calling card of death is life.*

34. *The longing for a permanent identity is the first refusal of love beyond the limits of belief.*

35. *The Hymn of Praise for the crown of thorns is the cross, robe, and sandals of one's own sacred karma.*

36. *Phenomena and sensation must be recognized as the transfiguration of change.*

37. *The divine inferno resounds with the benediction of communion.*

38. *To believe in the Holy of Holies is to create in oneself the desire to always be the infinite Bishop.*

39. *To surrender one's integrity to the transitory is to renounce the search for the miraculous.*

40. *The music of the spheres is a facade. It is the noise of the living flow that is the seed of real growth.*

41. *The automaticity of worship in the temple of stone is the chosen lot of those who have forgotten the anointing of the Almighty.*

42. *The automatic programs of habits can be broken only by substitution—new lamps for old.*

45) GUIDE No. 9, 1975   5"x7"

43. *Creation cannot be destroyed. It is maintained by the essence-habits even after the mind has died away.*

44. *Man is trapped by his habits—food, sex, and survival— but without them, where would he be?*

45. *Once you destroy the psyche, the light of the essence can never be turned off. So you had better be certain you want it before you ask for it.*

46. *I can only give you what you ask for—and you can only ask for what you need. If you want more, then make it necessary to your very existence.*

47. *The theology of self-gratification is to succumb to stupidity and desire, the game of the senses.*

48. *One must demand justice and learn to live without it.*

49. *How can you have a hungry desire for the absolute beingness of non-existence in the void and demand the company of your friends at the same time?*

50. *Essence-communication, or "telepathy", sensing and seeing from a distance, levitation, and the power to move the mountain are all the basis for real sacrifice. When the Lord asks you to sacrifice your firstborn, you must not offer up a substitute.*